"The Prosperity Plan leads you through a series of [...]
and wall-busting exercises. Laura is a master at di[...]
path to reach your personal definition of prosper[...]

entrepreneur, producer, wife, and mother of [...]

"Laura's deep wisdom and keen intuition about life and human behavior are unparalleled. This combined with her practical approach and great sense of humor make her a true master in her field. It was an honor to be a part of the *Prosperity Plan* program."

—ARJAN EENKEMA VAN DIJK,
executive coach

"The Prosperity Plan was just what I needed. The holistic approach was unique, challenging, and advantageous. Laura raised my consciousness so that I now understand what was holding me back and how to move forward. I feel more conscientious, grateful, and prosperous! Thank you."

—MERLE BENNY, Thinc. Creative

"My husband and I are both self-employed and have experienced our share of financial ups and downs. When I began the *Prosperity Plan* book/program, his business and our household income were at all-time lows. We were feeling a lot of stress around money, especially since our son's first college bills were looming. The book/program gave me a new and healthier perspective on money. It turned out that my shift into more of a prosperity consciousness was contagious. My husband's business picked up, and I'm continuing to attract new opportunities. Instead of worrying about money, I now trust that all will be well."

—GRACE DURFEE, PCC, PMC, RMT,
professional certified coach,
Usui Reiki master teacher,
author of *Balance with Grace: Celebrate the Kaleidoscope of Life*

"The Prosperity Plan helped me activate a lot of possibility within my life and business in a short amount of time—and during a period of difficult personal circumstances. With practical and simple (though not always easy!) steps, Laura guides you to greater prosperity in all forms (yes, including money!) very quickly and sustainably."

—PAULA GREGOROWICZ, The Paula G. Company

"*The Prosperity Plan* offers proven and powerful tools to shift your beliefs and manifest impressive outcomes. Do this program and watch your fortunes soar!"

—Nancy Collamer, mylifestylecareer.com

"The *Prosperity Plan* program exceeded my expectations in unexpected ways. What was different about this program is that it felt like a freeing and organic process instead of something I had to do or should do. The design was brilliant and enabled me to do the legwork, let go and watch the results just flow. I now feel more abundance and prosperity than ever."

—Nancy Friedberg, M.A., career expert

"*The Prosperity Plan* is your guide to the success secrets that blend the proven knowledge from yesterday with the spiritual demands of our times. Change your operating system via this plan and you will see the results you want."

—Sandy Vilas, MCC, CEO, Coach U.

"Once again, Laura B. Fortgang explains the balance between spiritual practice and grounded practicality. The guidelines in *The Prosperity Plan* work. My first clue happened thirteen years ago when I left a suffocating marriage. My three asthmatic children and I never had another asthma attack. Inspired, I diligently followed all of the principles that Laura B. Fortgang has so thoughtfully outlined for you in *The Prosperity Plan*. I now have an abundance of time, money, love, friends, adventure, and beauty in my life. I continue to invite prosperity into my life and it just keeps getting better."

—Denise Seiffer, CEO, Video Rental Services

"Have you ever met a CEO who says, 'No, we shouldn't do this, we're not good enough, smart enough, or strong enough'? I'm guessing, NO! Success and prosperity come from knowing that you can make anything happen.

"This book confirms what I have always felt in my gut. That much of my success, and those that I have seen succeed around me, has come from my strongly held beliefs that 'IT is possible.' Prosperity is within each of us.

"[*The Prosperity Plan*] will put you back in charge of your life by reminding you that you get to choose. I couldn't put it down, this is VITAL reading for anyone who wants to make their own good fortune happen. Read it and change your world."

—A. Hanson, COO, Academic Healthcare

THE PROSPERITY PLAN

∞

THE PROSPERITY PLAN

∞

*Ten Steps
to Beating the Odds and
Creating Extraordinary Wealth
(and Happiness)*

LAURA B. FORTGANG

JEREMY P. TARCHER/PENGUIN
a member of Penguin Group (USA) Inc.
New York

JEREMY P. TARCHER/PENGUIN
Published by the Penguin Group
Penguin Group (USA) Inc., 375 Hudson Street, New York, New York 10014,
USA • Penguin Group (Canada), 90 Eglinton Avenue East, Suite 700, Toronto, Ontario
M4P 2Y3, Canada (a division of Pearson Penguin Canada Inc.) • Penguin Books Ltd,
80 Strand, London WC2R 0RL, England • Penguin Ireland, 25 St Stephen's Green,
Dublin 2, Ireland (a division of Penguin Books Ltd) • Penguin Group (Australia),
250 Camberwell Road, Camberwell, Victoria 3124, Australia (a division of Pearson Australia
Group Pty Ltd) • Penguin Books India Pvt Ltd, 11 Community Centre, Panchsheel Park,
New Delhi–110 017, India • Penguin Group (NZ), 67 Apollo Drive, Rosedale, North
Shore 0632, New Zealand (a division of Pearson New Zealand Ltd) • Penguin Books
(South Africa) (Pty) Ltd, 24 Sturdee Avenue, Rosebank, Johannesburg 2196, South Africa

Penguin Books Ltd, Registered Offices: 80 Strand, London WC2R 0RL, England

Most Tarcher/Penguin books are available at special quantity discounts for bulk purchase
for sales promotions, premiums, fund-raising, and educational needs. Special books or
book excerpts also can be created to fit specific needs. For details, write Penguin Group
(USA) Inc. Special Markets, 375 Hudson Street, New York, NY 10014.

Library of Congress Cataloging-in-Publication Data

Fortgang, Laura Berman.
The prosperity plan : ten steps to beating the odds and creating extraordinary wealth
(and happiness) / Laura Berman Fortgang.
p.   cm.
ISBN 978-1-58542-856-4
1. Success in business.   2. Financial security.   3. Wealth—Psychological aspects.
4. Happiness.   I. Title.
HF5386.F457   2011   2010032581
650.1—dc22

Printed in the United States of America
1   3   5   7   9   10   8   6   4   2

BOOK DESIGN BY TANYA MAIBORODA

While the author has made every effort to provide accurate telephone numbers and Internet
addresses at the time of publication, neither the publisher nor the author assumes any
responsibility for errors, or for changes that occur after publication. Further, the publisher does
not have any control over and does not assume any responsibility for author or third-party
websites or their content.

CONTENTS

INTRODUCTION

The difference [between those that make money and
those who don't] is as much about doing as it is about
believing. It's about making your own luck.

—JEAN CHATZKY,
money journalist and motivational speaker

∞

THERE is a huge shift happening in the evolution of human consciousness. Are you feeling it? Is your world changing without your permission? Have you been forced to reinvent your work or give up things in your life you once held dear? But here is the good news: as frightening as it can be when things swing out of our control, it is in precisely in times like these that we begin to pay attention—and a dramatic shift in consciousness becomes possible. However, the choice to *remain* conscious is entirely up to you. You could also just hide and go back to sleep.

Whether you are picking up this book out of desperation or because you know that something is trying to emerge from within you, one thing is certain: global economic changes are forcing us to embrace a new way of building our lives and financial security. The old ways "guaranteed" by hard work, fitting in, and loyalty are no longer enough to ensure your career and give peace of mind about the future. We need a new currency that requires a rewiring of our minds and of our beliefs about how prosperity works. "Prosperity consciousness," the mind science of creating wealth, once thought of as merely a nice idea, will now need to become an integral part of human and social development.

The work I have done for almost twenty years as a pioneer in the personal coaching field has been grounded in the belief that, as John Naisbitt, futurist and author of *Megatrends* and *Megatrends 2000*, put it, "the most exciting breakthroughs of the 21st century will not occur because of technology but because of an expanding concept of what it means to be human." I interpret that to mean that our awareness of the spiritual nature of our being will become the currency of our future success. By subduing that aspect of ourselves despite all that we accomplished in the twentieth century, we inflicted unintended damage on our planet, our health, and other beings. We have seen our ever-expanding progress and prosperity begin to contract and many of our systems fall apart. The health of our environment is in danger as well as our social systems for caring for the sick, the elderly, and families in general. We've misplaced our security and want desperately to get it back. It is likely to come in a new form, however.

As modern luminaries in business call for innovation, creativity, and right-brain, out-of-the-box thinking to cure corporate ills, we are seeing the same need in every area of our individual and collective lives. Cutting-edge business thinkers are calling for this shift as the way for individuals and corporate entities to survive. They are not using spiritual language for this, but I will and I hope to prove that this is not just a mandate for the airy-fairy brigade. More and more, we will be seeing that our way of being has to change as the prerequisite to the changes in what we are doing. What we have done so far no longer seems to be working, so it is time to heed the call.

In her recent book *The Difference: How Anyone Can Prosper in Even the Toughest Times*, Jean Chatzky wrote of the results of a survey of 5,000 Americans that she commissioned with Harris Interactive with cooperation from Merrill Lynch. It was found that 3 percent of the group could be considered wealthy, defined as having at least $2 million in investible assets (not including the equity in their home), and that 27 percent were comfortable ($240,000 in investible assets), with the rest living on the edge (paycheck to paycheck) or completely in debt. What proved most interesting about this study was that the defining factors about what made the participants wealthy or comfortable was not so much about their knowledge of finances as much as it was about certain attitudes and beliefs.

Books such as *Think and Grow Rich* by Napoleon Hill, *The Science of Getting Rich* by Wallace D. Wattles, and *The Mental Equivalent: The Secret of Demonstration* by Emmet Fox—all written in the early 1900s through 1943—expound on the importance of attitude, belief, ambition, possibility, and often the belief in God. These texts have sold well for decades and still do.

What you will read here echoes some of what those books say, but you will be guided to what I hope is a more modern and updated understanding of where these giants wanted to lead you.

For me, money has always been a game to play. For years, when my kids were toddlers (they are now grade-schoolers), the game was to make the same amount of money every year by putting in less and less time. In my early earning years—starting when I was fourteen, making $2 an hour working at the local dry cleaner—the game was for me to pay for my own dance and voice lessons, and for gas for the car my parents lent me, and to save any money I could. In my twenties, the game was to save for a house (while I waited on tables and pursued an acting career and all the expenses involved with marketing myself then). I made a full 20 percent down payment on said house in cash. For a lot of people, I know, the game—not a fun one at that—is to just make it to the next paycheck.

So mine is not a story of how many millions I gained and

lost, but it *is* a story of how a middle-class kid who was not given a new car at seventeen and who contributed significantly to her own college education chose a life of self-employment with no lifeline other than the savings she had from waiting on tables—and how she went on to support others to make the money of their dreams while she earned hers.

I will flat-out tell you that I was more careful with my money when I had less of it. When I was doing summer stock theater in my early twenties for $40 a week, I managed to save money! When I worked on a cruise ship in 1987, I made $300 a week and saved 75 percent of it. When I bought my house and my business was growing, my husband and I saved at a rate that astounded our financial planner.

If you're a skeptic, you can say that my story was all luck. There were circumstances like a rent-stabilized apartment in New York City and steady work as a waitress and part-time actress, but there was also a lot of hard work and a focus on financial care that was almost hyperactive.

After three kids and a total loss of my husband's business after 9/11, the road got very bumpy. We had debt (other than a mortgage) for the very first time. We began to live beyond our means because we got caught with a big lifestyle and the loss of an income. None of it felt like a game anymore. I'm sure many of you can relate to that, considering recent times.

As the world grew more afraid, and the threat of terrorism—along with financial gloom and doom—started to rule the airwaves, I believe I unwittingly caught the bug. I did not realize, until I was out of it, that I lived in deep fear for the four years following 9/11. What that did to my ability to prosper was really awful. When I finally grasped what was happening, it was somewhat late. One of my children was suffering from the sudden onset of a seizure disorder (which one adviser intimated may have been connected to my own energetic terror at the time), and my fear only grew as medical bills and, more importantly, my son's uncertain future loomed over my head.

Miracles do happen, and my son was rendered seizure-free as suddenly and as unexpectedly as he was struck with the condition. In the time since, I have regained my mental footing and the ability to keep fear in its place. My husband's career did eventually rebound, and we keep growing and pruning our financial tree.

It may help to know that until recently, I was skeptical of prosperity consciousness teachings. My experience was that they worked for other people and not me. It made sense to me intellectually how it might work, but it was not my thing. However, having felt the squeeze of the almost back-to-back recessions since 2001, I began looking back at what had worked for me before. I started to study what I had done in those earlier years when life was less chaotic that made for all that "luck": my housing coups, the jobs turning up at the right times, meeting the man of my dreams, the rapid growth of my business—including an appearance on *The Oprah Winfrey Show*, all the national morning shows, the features in major magazines and newspapers—and so much more. What I realized was that I was doing what prosperity consciousness teaches without realizing it.

The difference between then and the years where things went wrong was my mental focus. I have always had setbacks, but I also had an unwavering focus on what I was trying to create and a naiveté that allowed me to carry on, undisturbed by naysayers.

Upon discovering this, I felt it was the perfect time to make prosperity consciousness a priority and to approach it systematically. A dear friend of mine and I became prosperity partners, encouraging each other and plotting action steps together. I hired a coach in this area and, for the first time, started to see the results that I had grown accustomed to earlier in my moneymaking life. My deep, unquestioning commitment was the key. And as I got further into the study of prosperity, I remembered that I made the most magically successful leaps over the course of my life when I was following the principles you will master here.

What are your expectations right now? Are you fearful and worried? Are you concerned that the changes in the world preclude ever feeling on top of your game again? Are you resisting what is going on in your life?

If you are living in this currency of fear, you are putting your feet in a tub of wet cement and letting it harden into a solid block. Your movements and your ability to change will be limited.

However, if you work through the Prosperity Plan, you will find that you can create results similar to the ones I did. I have written this book so it can work for you, so *you* can experience way-above-average to truly extraordinary. By creating the circumstances by which great luck can find you, you will experience prosperity and opportunity that is magical in quality. Sometimes it will be sudden, sometimes it will take longer than you would like, but by mastering the principles, you *will* get results. You will be the one to beat the odds.

To get you there, this book is organized as an acronym for P-R-O-S-P-E-R-I-T-Y. Each chapter will guide you to adopt and master the principles, skills, and mind-set that will result in putting your life on the path to prosperity and happiness. There will be suggested actions to take to get the desired results: Take them! Follow each chapter in order and take on what it suggests. At the end, you'll be left with a master plan to put your new mind-set into action in the world.

Along the way, there will be stories to inspire you that were culled from interviews with clients, friends, and strangers who have overcome obstacles to prosper financially. Most of them are millionaires and gladly shared their experiences with me to pass on to you.

By embarking on the journey that this book will take you on, you are agreeing to rewire the way you think about money and creating opportunity in your life. The prosperity principles herein are not new, but the reasons for adopting them *now* are unprecedented in their importance and urgency. To succeed, a fundamental change is required of you. You will be recalibrating your energy and vibration level, and keeping that going means staying conscious and allowing yourself to grow. It will mean doing conscious battle with your subconscious and it will mean anchoring yourself in the better half of your thinking. When fear, doubt, or your critical voice try to intervene, you'll have to send them out to pasture. To keep yourself in the right mind-set, read this material repeatedly or read any text that keeps you in tune with your best self and infinite wisdom.

Welcome to the Prosperity Plan. To beat the odds and attain the level of wealth and happiness you have always dreamed of, you will have to "play to win." You have nothing to lose and everything to gain.

Chapter 1

POSSIBILITY

*Become a possibilitarian. No matter how
dark things seem to be or actually are, raise your
sights and see possibilities—always see them,
for they're always there.*

—NORMAN VINCENT PEALE

Wʜᴇʀᴇ do you live? In your mind, I mean. Do you live in "the Land of Possibility"?

Perhaps you're more inclined to live in "the Land of Fear, Doubt and Media Saturation." Think about it. Where are you mentally inclined to focus? If you're like most people, you have a strong linear and logical mind that does not have a lot of patience for imagination. You're likely to be better tuned in to your critical brain than your daydreaming side. Right? The good news is you're not alone. The bad news is you have a lot of work ahead of you to pack up your mental house and move from one side of your brain to the other. Out of the critic and into the dreamer—pronto!

You are reading this book to increase prosperity, so let's use the analogy of investments. If you make bad investments, you get bad results. If you make good investments, you prosper. Which would you rather invest in: your mind that keeps you believing in the limits you see (which may be very real, to be sure), or the mind that sees a shiny future? Where will you invest? Honestly, do you have a choice? You have to invest in the possibilities, even if they seem improbable based on current circumstances.

This sounds like positive-thinking, fluffy mumbo jumbo, doesn't it? Well, that's 'cause it is! I ask you: And what's wrong with that? We are not talking about denial. We are not talking about ignoring the facts. But we *are* talking about opening up room for good things to happen and money to come to you by seeing opportunity where most see roadblocks. We are about to tap into the potential you have to create new circumstances for yourself and those you care about. We are setting you up to beat the odds. Being wealthy is a possibility for you if you are able to overcome your own limits to seeing that as true.

I'd like you to consider the source. I am a recovering perfectionist and former black-and-white thinker. In my earlier life there were no shades of gray, or even color. Things were good or bad. Right or wrong. Maybe it's more truthful to say things were either fabulous or devastating. The highs did not last long and the lows were habit. Sheer habit that festered and grew and multiplied into a severe depression. The ensuing years of daily discipline (which gets easier year by year, by the way) have produced a new, more balanced version of my former self, without all my negative tendencies—a version that is a testament to keeping your mind out of the toilet. Having been to hell and back, I can say with authority that "the Land of Possibility" feels much better and yields better results.

What most of us do is get stuck in what is probable and likely to occur. We watch the newscasts and read the news with great interest in order to remain informed, despite it being common knowledge that newscasts need ratings, so they have to scare you up until the commercial breaks to be sure you stay put to hear still more bad news afterward. You need information to make smart choices in your life, but there is no such thing as "fair and balanced" news, and there is no governing party making sure that you receive the same amount of bad and good news. You get mostly bad news and that is what you base your life decisions on. Is it any wonder that most people don't prosper? They are not feeding themselves the right brain food! What we consume in information affects our prosperity. When you are offered— and eat—tidbit after tidbit laced with fear and presented with enough authority to convince you that failure or loss is the probable outcome, then you are limited. You are. Only when you keep your sights on what is possible, despite the odds, do you multiply your chances of beating those odds.

How this works has everything to do with our subconscious mind and unseen spiritual elements. Science tells us that the subconscious is a collection of all the impressions we have taken in since we were infants. The subconscious does not know whether what it receives is good or bad for us, but it does register our most repeated thoughts as truth. And often, despite our best conscious efforts to the contrary, our subconscious mind does not change and our results stay the same.

We think in three ways: (1) via our conscious mind, the cognitive part that is aware and purposeful in its process; (2) subconscious thinking, which is a collection of learning, training, and functions (like how our body works with no conscious help from us, or how, with experience, we can drive a car without consciously focusing); and (3) the superconscious, which simply *knows* and is the consciousness of the ethers and nature. It is known by many names: the Divine Mind, God, the Universe, Nature, Source, All That "Is," the Higher Self. It does not matter what it's called; what's important is that both science and spirituality have acknowledged it as the mastermind behind the alchemy of creating something from nothing. It is connected to all things, seen and unseen, and has a limitless capacity. It knows no boundaries.

To retrain your subconscious is a key element of the Prosperity Plan. You will have to spend a lot of time being mindful of the conscious mind and the superconscious. As you do, you will start to change how you feel about yourself, your circumstances, and the possibilities about what you can create and accomplish. Feeling this in your body is the recalibration this book will help you achieve, and it is that recalibration that will get the lead out of your subconscious and program it for better results.

According to Pandit Shriram Sharma Acharya, a Hindu sage who pioneered a scientific approach to spirituality, the law of the persistence of energy causes the contrast between the levels of consciousness. The more energy an individual spends on one form of consciousness, the less he can spend on another. So, if we spend a lot of time in an upset state (fear, anxiety, worry), we have less energy for action and pursuing what's possible. The superconscious mind, like the subconscious, cannot discern whether the messages sent to it are good or bad. Its job is just to manifest them. It simply acts on whatever energy it receives, attracting more of the like energy and starting the process of bringing into being. The universe is like one big mirror, giving you back what you project into it. It wants to say yes to you, and it does. "I don't make enough money!" thrown into the mirror comes back as "YES! You do not make enough money! Isn't that ducky? Here is more of the same!"

The problem is that most of the time people want something desperately in their conscious mind, yet in their subconscious mind they have intense emotion concentrated on what they don't want or distaste for what they currently have.

Our voluntary, or conscious, desires and wishes cannot persevere through the weight of the automatic thinking of the subconscious.

Let's take a work scenario as an example. You have a job and know that's a good thing, but you spend most of your time thinking fearful thoughts about losing that job, or how hard it will be for you to put up with it over the long term, or how much you dislike the people you have to interact with. But you don't look for other work because you are complacent and glad to have a paycheck. What you keep broadcasting to your superconscious is how unhappy you are, so more scenarios come up to make you unhappy. You start causing tension in the workplace, and as soon as there are layoffs and staff cuts, you are let go. You are shocked, dismayed, and upset. However, on closer inspection, you have to admit that you were asking to be let go for a long time—you just did not have the courage to take the initiative yourself. As you kept broadcasting your disdain, the superconscious kept sending it back to you for a volley of Ping-Pong until a situation manifested itself. You did not consciously intend to get yourself fired, but your subconscious did the work for you through the power of your fears.

What we know from quantum physics and the work of Masaru Emoto is that our world is composed of energy and that we can funnel that energy for our own good. Researchers like Dr. Emoto, who has studied the energy contained in water and its crystals when frozen, have discovered that subatomic particles act and respond in exact proportion to the thoughts or expectations of the people who are conducting the studies. The energy around us will respond to the vibrational energy of our own thinking. This is what we are going to harness in the Prosperity Plan.

If you've ever gone to work or a gathering of some kind in a fantastic mood and then, within an hour, noticed that your mood disintegrated until it was like that of the people around you, you have experienced your energy level and your body's vibration lowered to match theirs.

Bruce H. Lipton, Ph.D., author of *The Biology of Belief: Unleashing the Power of Consciousness, Matter & Miracles*, explains in his work how cells, beginning with the most basic life forms, speak to each other and sense each other, responding to unseen elements that prompt growth. The energy of nature combined with the thinking brain, crude or sophisticated, is designed for growth and increase. It's designed for good. For us, it starts here with experiencing "the Land of Possibility," where your vibration energy of possibility can respond in kind to the energy from the universe and bring the growth and increase you are trying to create into a tangible reality.

In his book, Lipton says: "The latest science leads us to a worldview not unlike that held by the earliest civilizations, in which every material object in Nature was thought to possess a spirit. . . . All are imbued with . . . [this] spirit, the invisible energy. . . . This is the world of quantum physics, in which matter and energy are completely entangled." This is the invitation that is being extended to you. It is to recognize the connection in yourself to everything in the universe that will help you attain your deepest desires while creating a sustainable kind of wealth that goes back out into time and space to help others do the same. Achievement through the harnessing and honoring of spirit is central to the Prosperity Plan. It is low-impact, it is "green," and it is extraordinarily powerful. So are you. This is a chance to rise above your instinctual nature to doubt, complain, fear, and believe in the illusion of ill fate. As you gradually transform your nature, you will see your circumstances change.

You probably hoped that the Prosperity Plan would be easy. Well, it can be, but only once the hard work is done. And this hard work is nothing like the usual idea of hard work involving a lot of time and sweat. This hard work is about changing your operating system. It is equally hard, but you're working in a different dimension. It is the dimension of spirit and your own evolution.

By *evolution*, I mean coming into a higher level of awareness; in this case, that awareness is about your capacity to create wealth in your life and your ability to operate in a new mind-set of loving creation instead of the old mind-set of "survival of the fittest." Creation and collaboration will usher out the competitive model. You are being called to heal yourself, your world, and the world at large through whatever you create next. This is the spiritual evolution that is at hand. Your prosperity will no longer be at the expense of someone else's. What's more, your effect on others will further enhance your ability to achieve what you long for.

Are you still resisting being a "possibilitarian"? Unless you majored in probability and statistics in college, you should be as equipped as the next person to adapt to possibility. The only difference between you and everyone else is your willingness.

If you want the Prosperity Plan to work for you, you must be willing to convince every fiber of your being of what is possible. That willingness must take root and become an integral part of who you are. Now.

To Activate Possibility:

- Commit to keeping the impact of the media and other fearful influences at a minimum, if not eliminating them completely.
- Write down specifics about the kinds of prosperity you want to create: financial, romantic, material, professional, or all of these. (*Making more money* is not specific; *increasing my income by $5,000 by June 1* is specific.)
- Write down any examples of how just your power of thinking was enough to cause a change or something significant to happen in your life.

❈ List the times in your life when something you thought was impossible or unlikely actually happened.

❈ List the occasions when you had proof that you could connect to other people just by thinking about them (for example, you thought of them and they called, or you knew you'd run into them when you had no previous knowledge of their whereabouts.

❈ Take everything you just recorded and use it to empower a new list, titled "It Is Possible That":

1. *I am making $5,000 a month more this year.*

2. *I find everything I need to start my new venture.*

3. *I have a home I love in a place I love.*

4. *I am a millionaire by the time I am fifty.*

❈ Read this list aloud every day, twice a day, as you work through the Prosperity Plan.

Chapter 2

RIGHT LIVELIHOOD

*Always leave enough time in your life to do
something that makes you happy, satisfied, even
joyous. That has more of an effect on economic
well-being than any other single factor.*

—PAUL HAWKEN,
environmentalist, entrepreneur and author

STRETCHING our capacity beyond the limits of our current
habits and beliefs brings us to the concept of "right livelihood." The term comes from the ancient Buddhist "Eight-
Fold Path," but it is the most up-to-date strategy I can think
of for getting on a path to prosperity in today's world. With
half of the U.S. workforce still dissatisfied with their jobs it
seems only likely that living in a state of frustration and ennui
is hampering one's ability to prosper despite actually having an income. Living in a tornado of inner chaos in order
to make an income is not one's "right" livelihood. The true
pathway to joyous monies will come from what the Buddhists

call one's dharma, and it is a path that is in service to others. In fact, as Mahatma Gandhi said: "The best way to find yourself is to lose yourself in the service of others."

In *Awakening the Buddha Within: Tibetan Wisdom for the Western World*, Lama Surya Das quotes the Dhammapada, an ancient scripture, when he says: "Right Livelihood is said to be 'in tune with increasing helpfulness for being and decreasing harmfulness.' It asks us to love our world through our work."

In our modern society, the path to riches through enterprise grew from monopolies that brought much-needed progress and industrialization to the world. It was a dizzying time of prosperity as everyone became better off by being part of an industrialized world. By now you know that this era has run its course. We've damaged the planet, we've seen greed crumbling stability, and we've seen our jobs replaced by machines or become irrelevant altogether. The dot-com boom was not what it promised to be, either.

Our progress has now rendered any work that can be done by a machine or "outsourced" dispensable. But you are not dispensable when you contribute what you were built to do. On our path to prosperity, the question has to change from "How am I going to make money?" to "What am I built to do and how do I monetize that?" Think of all the people you know who have asked the first question; then think of how many of them are happy and enjoying their choice. I'm sure some are, but I know most aren't, because I've worked with them or met them at lectures or they make up the 50 percent of the people who statistics say would switch careers if given the chance. Prosperity flows where your "great joy meets the world's needs," as the theologian and ordained Presbyterian minister Frederick Buechner says.

Having grown up watching TV, images from shows I've seen often come up for me as metaphors for life. One that has been showing up in my mind's eye for many years is the prairie town in Wisconsin where author Laura Ingalls Wilder, whose work inspired the television series *Little House on the Prairie,* grew up. The town was scant, with a schoolhouse, a mercantile area, and a few other buildings where services were provided by the town doctor or maybe the tinker. That image has served as a symbol for where I've sensed the world of work headed. I have long felt that we will be going backward a bit to recapture the essence of work, with each person clearly filling a need in the community. As we shift from competition as the operating system of life and work to one of cooperation, a small society makes it easier to see how each person adds to the whole. That image of the small, simple town mirrors what I see happening to work today. We are being forced, some by economics and some by our own spiritual evolution, to seek our unique contribution to the world. We are ready to get back to giving our unique offering to make the world work better and to support our lives. This is what dharma is.

There are many bumper-sticker-type slogans out there urging you to "live your bliss." You've heard them: "Do what you love and the money will follow." "Live your passion!" "Live your purpose!" I think there is truth in those statements, but the pain these platitudes cause people tells me there has to be more to it. I know of so many people who suffer or have anxiety over not having found that one thing that is their passion—that which will make them happy and make them money.

I don't believe there is only one form that your right livelihood, passion, or purpose must take. There are many ways that it can be expressed. What has become clear to me after years of working with people so that they may recognize their purpose and right work is that it is not a matter of one project, passion, or job; rather, it is a way of being, a talent, a unique attribute you have that cannot be repeated by anyone, because no one else can be you. And that quality or strength expressed through you can fit into a myriad of job descriptions.

Ultimately, it is not what you do that will make you happy but how you feel when you are doing it. Who it allows you to be is the secret to the joy.

Chances are, there is a theme that has followed you throughout your life and through different jobs. Until it is discovered, named, and brought into your awareness, it will never register with you as being important. When you identify it, name it, and see how it has always been a part of you, you will have confirmation that you are supposed to amplify that part of yourself and allow it to be the criterion for your choice of work. The part that matters is that the fullest expression of you be made accessible to you. It is then that you will experience the joy that fosters prosperity. You will be contributing what you were built to contribute. So I'd change the motto "Do what you love, and the money will follow" to "The money will follow when you work with love."

You don't have to know *what* you love to do to do that. You just have to become the person you've always wanted to *be* right where you are and watch how your work will transform. You will make different choices. You will be given different opportunities. You may leave your current work or you'll be released from it and be free to pursue avenues where you can be who you want to be. Just be who you truly are through your work, no matter what it is, and you will be living in the vibration that attracts the most money to you. Use what you are blessed with and the world gets to benefit—it's a prosperity-making formula.

I know what your inner critic is probably saying: "Yeah, that's nice, but I still hate my job." Or you may be thinking,

"If I don't stay here, how do I pay my mortgage?" There are certainly mitigating factors and concrete realities to negotiate. Nonetheless, a state of worry and anxiety caused by any circumstance is not the most conducive to sustainable prosperity. And yet, any new venture or temporary lapse in income is nerve-wracking and anxiety producing. A catch-22. What to do? Mostly, that negative cycle is the result of being trained to think that losing a job is a tragedy and that attempting something new is asking for failure. Neither has to be true, but we are so deeply conditioned to accept those common notions that we don't even try, once again shutting off the source of prosperity. People who get rich when they face these scenarios do so because they understand they are stepping into a plan for their greatest prosperity without waiting for the circumstances to show that they are right before they even start out. Prosperity does not grow from doubt: it grows from certainty before you even see results. (More on that in Chapter 4, "Security.")

What if losing a job were an opportunity to reclaim a part of you that you once cast aside to keep a paycheck? What if starting a business were the first time that you felt you were making a difference, even if you had to get by on less money to start? Feeling alive and taking risks are part of the Prosperity Plan. It's back to living in *possibility*, an outlook you should already be on your way to adopting. Yes, money to pay the bills is critical. But as I said in the previous chapter, we are not talking about denial: we are talking about getting on a path to right livelihood despite the many obstacles you perceive as deal breakers.

I had the opportunity to hear the Reverend Michael Beckwith tell a story about his work choices. Beckwith is a popular New Thought minister in California who has reached national recognition through his work. He tells the story of his earlier days as a government employee and how he was laid off and unemployed for a period of nine months. During that time, he scrimped and did jobs here or there that brought in a little money. He was doing his due diligence in his job search and eventually was presented with an offer to head a government agency, his dream job. At about the same time, he was given the opportunity to take on a full-time role in his church, teaching the principles he so cherished. He had to choose which way to go. He could not do both, since the church job required traveling. The dream job carried the title and the money he had been hoping for, but the church position allowed him to be who he truly wanted to be.

Michael had just been through nine months of scraping by, which he would have to keep doing on the church job's lower pay. As he tells it, he chose his destiny over his dream job, and that path put him on the journey to where he is today. He is wealthy and loves being who he really is, without boundaries and limits, while serving countless people around the globe.

I also recently had a chance to catch up with John Harvey,

whose story I often tell at my lectures as the story of "the Fish-monger." John is a lovely man who read my book *Now What? 90 Days to a New Life Direction* and who, in a chance meeting backstage at an NBC TV show appearance in New York City, told me about his journey to his right livelihood. He had been a white-collar executive in financial services and was shocked to learn he was being let go. He was in his mid-fifties and found it almost impossible to land another similar job. After two years of being unemployed, and with his savings close to running out, he was approached by a local fish store owner in town who told him he had once been a white-collar guy like him; he had run the local fish market for many years, how-ever, and was ready to sell it. He wondered if John would like to buy it from him.

"Be a fishmonger?" John was surprised, and taken aback. "I'm a white-collar executive, I'm not a fishmonger."

Well, the idea kept eating at him, and despite every logi-cal reason he could think of and the fears about what people would think and how his kids would adjust to a smaller house and public (versus private) school, John bought the business.

As it turned out, he loved his work. He loved how he got to see his kids every day, which he had not done when he was an executive. His kids cared more about having him around than they did about private school or their old, bigger home, and he prided himself on running his business with integrity and serving his community.

John sold the business four years later, after learning many lessons about business and teamwork, and now uses those skills as a consultant to large organizations. He also runs seminars for displaced executives looking to take their next steps. John's children miss the fishmonger years, and he has no regrets, because he was enriched and freed to live a life oriented around what he valued instead of being confined in a box shrouded by external expectations.

Right livelihood is about aligning your actions with your soul's calling. It is about becoming the kind of person you want to be and expressing it through the work that you do. And this work will, inevitably, be something that ultimately benefits others, be it in the form of a service or product you provide that helps people or just by making a living in a way that is respectful of the rest of humanity. Right livelihood is about embracing your solitary uniqueness and allowing it to be a channel through which love can exist and flourish in the world.

I am frequently asked how I got myself on some of the most popular television shows to talk about my books and how someone might pursue the same path that I did. Sure, you can hire a publicist and spend lots of money trying to get the media's attention, but there is no guarantee that will work. There is also another way: you can do your best work with all your heart and soul, give people what they need, and see how the word spreads. You will build a reputation such that when you do put yourself in front of traditional media (if you still choose to), you have your passion, track record, and following to take you all the way. People don't want to hear that answer. They want a name (which I don't have!), an in, or a shortcut. They want fame and fortune and see the work itself as a means to that end instead of the work being the point. I don't begrudge anyone their financial due, but I hope to drum home that your "right" work is what will get you the prosperity you desire. It's the work that will make you happy.

To Align with Your Right Livelihood

- What do you know in your heart you are supposed to be doing with your life? However large or small of a stretch it might be, just write it down. (It's okay, you don't have to show anyone just yet.)
- Alternatively, write down the dream you once had but did not pursue. Explore in writing if it is still applicable to who you are today and, if so, why.
- If that dream no longer works for you, explore the possibility that it might just be a metaphor for something that could be expressed through your work now. Also, explore if the real reason behind wanting to pursue that dream reflects who you want to be in the world. If so, that is the piece to fold into your life moving forward.

❀ Start *immediately* being more of *who* you are, despite the pressure your job description causes to the contrary.

❀ Practice the discipline of "right livelihood" in your attitude and choices daily.

❀ Sketch out an action plan showing how you could move further into your right livelihood over the next year.

Chapter 3

OPPORTUNITY

Most successful men have not achieved their
distinction by having some new talent or
opportunity presented to them. They have
developed the opportunity that was at hand.

—BRUCE MARTON

INVITING prosperity means seeing opportunity at every turn. It means knowing how to look for it and how to leverage what you already have so it yields results.

It is a completely proactive and action-oriented process and is rooted in the faith that comes from living in "possibility." Opportunity is as much a matter of perspective as anything else. There are fine points and it requires persistence. Discernment is required to know what really is an opportunity and what isn't. That discernment becomes more sophisticated as you grow more comfortable with your own intuition, which is the magic elixir that ties it all together.

It is hard to see opportunity when it is not obvious and

presented to you in the perfect package. It's likely that the first time a black pearl was discovered, it was cast away as a reject until it was later recognized as rare and valuable. The same goes for opportunity. Most people ignore it. Most people fear it if it is unproven. Most people don't take the time to connect with what shows up in their life and feel their way through the encounter. Most people are blind to the vehicles for opportunity that cross their path every day.

It's how you look at it. It's a matter of stepping into the mind-set and physical condition that I call "conductivity," which we will build on throughout this book. We have already begun to activate this conductivity, your ability to usher positive results into your life by working on living in possibility and pursuing your right livelihood. As we proceed, we need to focus on conductivity, a connection to your own body that allows you to feel what is right or wrong for you. You have this ability. It includes intuition, no doubt, but it also embraces a great truth: *The body never lies.*

Your body tells you when things are not right. You experience physical pain if something begs your attention health-wise. It also contracts when you are doing something you don't really want to do. When you are agonizing over a problem, your body is not comfortable and probably slumped over and less than positively aligned: it is trying to tell you something. When some place gives you the creeps and you leave, it's because your body just told you to get out. So conductivity involves moving your decision-making process from your head, where logical, linear thinking occurs, and extending it to include the signals from your body. Feeling your way through things rather than thinking your way through them becomes your best means for sensing opportunity.

Ali Brown is a self-made millionaire and an Inc. 500–ranked entrepreneur. She started out in her twenties working as an advertising copywriter—a job that her family and friends felt she was lucky to have—and was making $30,000 a year amid the glamour of New York City. But one day, as she stood on a street corner and noticed a homeless person and a limo within feet of each other, it dawned on Ali that life was all about choices and that hers was staring her in the face at that very moment. If she wanted to be as wealthy as she dreamed of being, it was not going to be by pursuing the career path she was on. That experience helped her decide that she would start her own copywriting business.

Over a period of five years, Ali's business grew from a struggling service business to a series of companies—coaching, publishing, and products—that support and teach business owners how to succeed. Often asked how she was making it on her own, she realized there was a whole market of women, especially, who needed help in order to succeed in their own companies. As she told me her story, she talked about how intuition plays a huge role in her life. She admits to using intuition ten times more than she uses logic and that her body was her barometer for making her first leap.

"It felt better to leave the firm I worked for and risk going out on my own than it did to stay," she says.

Seeing opportunity where others may not, very much depends on you honoring what your body is telling you and then acting on it. It involves courage. It takes openness. It often involves doing what may seem out of character for you. On closer examination, what may seem out of character may actually be your deepest values and desires finally pushing you out of your comfort zone. It's also likely that as you begin to voice what you are thinking of doing, people will tell you you're crazy. That's usually a darn good sign you are on the right track!

Our egos often get in the way of the opportunity life is trying to put in our path. We might feel something is beneath our station or has not shown up in the form we had expected, so we reject it. There are certainly times for high standards, but when you are shaking trees to create prosperity, at least at the beginning, everything is fair game. Eventually you will have new criteria for your prosperity journey, but at this point in your personal evolution, everything is game.

How your mind and ego will try to get in your way reminds me of a well-known story. . . .

A man climbs to the roof of his home to escape a flood

that is now reaching his second-floor windows. He prays for God to send help. A man on an inflatable raft comes by and offers to share it with the man on the roof. He refuses the offer and waits for God's help. A man with a rowboat comes by and offers him a trip to safety. The man on the roof thanks him and sends him on his way because God is sending him help. Next, a helicopter hovers over the man's home and throws a rope down to him. He waves the helicopter by, saying, "No, thanks," because help is on the way. Unfortunately, the man drowns, and when he meets his maker at the pearly gates, he asks: "I prayed for help—why didn't you send it?" God answers: "First I sent an inflatable raft, then a rowboat, then a helicopter. What more do you want from me?!"

In all fairness, there will be times when you are not sure what is an opportunity and you can't decipher what you are feeling. Fear can feel like excitement too. Nervousness can feel like elation. Anticipation can make you feel sick and be interpreted as a bad sign. The challenge is to learn to pay attention to your body and its more subtle feelings.

Learning to understand the signals your body sends you comes through practice. You simply begin to raise your awareness to include how you feel as one of your criteria for how you proceed in life. If it doesn't feel right, don't do it. If your body says no, so do you. Even if you think you do this already, I'm sure there is room to take it up a notch.

It's my experience and that of many who I have taught

over the years that fear is more jarring and disruptive to your senses and nervous system than excitement is. When intuition and your centered self are trying to speak to you, it is a feeling of expansion that comes over you versus the feeling of contraction that you get when your muscles tighten in the face of fear.

It may even help to take in a distinction you might find surprising at first. In her book *Your Invisible Power*, Genevieve Behrend suggests that excitement, usually thought of as a positive emotion, is actually a reflection of a belief in lack. Meaning that when you are excited about an outcome or a possibility, you are telegraphing that you would not expect such a good thing to be possible for you under normal circumstances. Shocking to our common wisdom, but with closer review, you will see that a true expectation that good things are destined for you, would not require excitement, but rather a calm knowing and acknowledgment of your rightful good fortune. Gratitude would be called for.

One of my prosperity students, Paula, shared an image that brought this into focus. Excitement is like a small dog jumping up and down, spinning and twirling to welcome you home, while gratitude is a graceful cat curling up to you on the couch, acknowledging your presence. I find this insight very helpful in recognizing a centered feeling in my body that indicates a "rightness" of an opportunity put in front of me.

What takes some sophistication, which you *will* develop

over time, is deciphering what is a true opportunity and what is just a seduction of some kind. By "seduction," I mean something that looks really good on the surface but may not result in the outcome you most want. Sometimes the emotional cost will be too high to say it's truly an opportunity. Be honest: How many times have you felt in your body that something was not quite right in the face of an opportunity and you moved ahead anyway, only to find at a point down the road that your original bad feeling was justified? Under the Prosperity Plan you are recalibrating your energetic vibration to attract money and flow in your life. If something is not conducive to that vibration, you will feel it, and it is critical that you pay attention.

Recognizing opportunity is just one part of the equation. The other part entails creating opportunity for yourself where there was no evidence of any previously. As unpleasant as the thought may be, you sometimes have to be willing to make a fool of yourself to create opportunity. What I mean is that you may have to be willing to be a student, to be more curious, to ask "dumb" questions, to call people you have no formal introduction to, or to claim a stake for what you want that is not popular or understood at first. In short, you have to become obsessed—at least to the point of having a burning desire to create the outcome you want. This is where the specifics you came up with in Chapter 1 come into play: these are the navigation aids you carry with you every day in your quest for opportunity, just as an early explorer would have looked for clues that he was nearing the undiscovered shores he had set out to find. My friend Wayne Madsen is a great example of the commitment, passion, desire, and specific goals that are needed to create opportunity. I met Wayne one January in a jury duty holding tank, waiting to perform our civic duty. We were both tapping away at our computers, and with one quick look at his screen I knew he was writing a book. So was I. We started talking and learned that the difference between us was that I was established as an author and he was not. He had written a children's book based on a story he told his daughter and son, called *The Misadventures of Inspector Moustachio*, which would soon be published by a small publisher whom he had persuaded to buy his book. He was doing his final rewrites that day.

The key word here is *convinced*. Wayne is a dentist by profession, and I have never met anyone more determined to make his dream of having a series of books that become a merchandisable brand come true. As I write this, Wayne, three years after we met, is signing a deal for the development of a television series and merchandising of his books. (There are now four stories about Inspector Moustachio!)

Here is what it took.

Wayne started this whole journey as a bet with his son, Jake. He was struggling with a writing assignment, and in a moment of frustration as Wayne tried to help him, he challenged his father on how much he knew about writing.

"You've never written anything!" he said.

Wayne came back with a deal.

"Fine. You get your grades up in writing, and I'll prove anyone can write by doing a book about Inspector Moustachio and getting it published and made into a movie!"

Wayne took on his own challenge with a vengeance as part of what he also deemed a midlife crisis. He wanted to prove that he could do something "out of the box," as he called it.

Wayne took to the Internet and entered a new writer's contest. He also pushed to get the attention of an agent or a publisher. He met with so many rejections that he was ready to give up until he read the book to his son's third-grade class and saw how much the kids loved it. He looked into self-publishing but was not ready to incur the cost of doing it on his own, so he persevered. He decided to change his cover letter from an amusing introduction of himself and the story behind the book to a more businesslike explanation of the book's moneymaking potential. Immediately the responses started to come in.

After many rejections from publishers, Wayne persuaded a small, independent press that his idea for a kids' book series was a worthwhile investment.

He had not quite intended to write a series until it came

out of his mouth as he pitched the book to the publisher. She produced the first book and Wayne ran with it. He, a neophyte when it came to marketing a book, spent countless hours on Amazon.com taking advantage of the blogging software to build an audience of readers, who in turn wrote rave reviews about his book. He sent his book to Barbara Bush, who has always had interest in promoting literacy. He decided while he was at it to also send it to Laura Bush, whose husband was in office at the time. His efforts resulted in his book appearing on a nationally published list of summer reading recommendations (the Reading Is Fundamental list) from the First Lady alongside many *New York Times*–bestselling authors. Wayne leveraged that coup by rallying his publisher to publish his second book in the series and by building momentum with this win. He also spent $3,000 of his own money to buy a link on Amazon.com (his publisher would not spring for it) to have his book come up as a recommended additional purchase link to a very popular children's book at the time.

Soon after, using the reading list as a bragging right, Wayne entered the book in a contest by iParenting. He did not win. The rejection only spurred him further. When he applied the second year, he entered the two Inspector Moustachio books— and won! By now iParenting was owned by Disney, which sent out national press releases about the winners and promoted the books on the iParenting website. Now Wayne was really fired up: he rallied his publisher to produce and release the third book in the series, which also eventually won an iParenting award.

Wayne did all this without an agent or any connections in the world of books. He asked anyone who'd listen what they knew about publishing and then about making in-roads in Hollywood. He did meet an agent through friends, but he still did legwork of his own. He researched online and found a list of Hollywood producers who packaged projects like his for television or movies. He wrote to every single one. He got on the phone and followed up. He even got a few responses and learned from the guidance those pros gave him. They all asked if he had a script for a movie. "Of course!" he said, then proceeded to crank one out in a weekend while poring over *Screenwriting for Dummies* and other how-to books.

After one false start, Wayne is now on his way with a company that is preparing to get his dream onto a small screen near you. His screenplay will be cut up into smaller episodes for TV. If everything goes as he envisions it, he will be making a career change and working closely with the production of his dream.

Most people don't have the stamina that Wayne has, and that is often why their dreams don't come true. Your dream for prosperity requires a daily burning passion in order to create the opportunities by which it will come to you, but keep in mind that we all have different limits to what we can do before we harm our sense of well-being. For example, Wayne's boundless energy burns even *me* out, but he is a great model of what it often takes to achieve the success you seek.

What Wayne did and what you can do with whatever you are creating and desiring is to start with what you have. Working with the skills and experience you already possess is essential to turning the tide in your direction. It is when you become paralyzed out of fear or wait for something to happen without taking any action that you risk getting even more deeply stuck. Remember, your subconscious will be happy to weigh you down. You have to keep your conscious mind connected to what's possible and tethered to the super-conscious.

Even if you feel stymied and sense that circumstances are stacked up against you, there is a place to start that will spark glimmers of opportunity for prosperity. Begin right where you are. If you see nothing good showing up, you need to first change your mind-set to see good. Stop dwelling on what you might lack and start noticing what you do have, even if it's not what you want exactly. Again, it's essential to start working with what you have.

Sometimes the first step is to get rid of or stop doing something that may be holding you back, before it's time to make something new happen. A surefire way to catalyze positive change is to throw away old junk. Literally and figuratively. Clear that desk, get that car washed, empty that closet, fire that problem employee despite any stress that will cause, and stop calling people who are naysayers in your life right now. In other words, create opportunity by creating a vacuum of space. When you make room, new things appear. You have proof of this, I'm sure. Have you ever cleared a counter in your home, only to have it cluttered again within a few days? Case in point. More room to put stuff—more stuff shows up. So, do that for your whole life! Now! Make room, make space, and you will invite opportunity.

Once you see the flow of opportunities begin, and once you've followed through on many of them, it will be time to develop the criteria I was alluding to earlier for determining which opportunities will help you prosper. Financial potential is not the only factor. It's about deciphering what is an opportunity and what is a distraction or a waste of time. The truth is that it's trial and error at first, especially if your specific goals are still a little fuzzy. When you are very clear on what you want to create (a dollar amount, a job, a contract for a movie deal), it's easier to know the difference. Nonetheless, this is exactly where your body's conductivity comes into place.

When Wayne entered the Hollywood stage of his journey, he met a producer who wanted to make a deal with him that did not feel right at all. Wayne knew the deal was not what he really wanted. However, he was tempted to go with it because it was Hollywood knocking and he was anxious that another chance might not come. At first he got caught up in the excitement of being wanted by Hollywood, but he recognized that he'd come too far on his own to agree to a standard contract for a writer. He wanted to be involved and have creative control. By conventional thinking, it was to his benefit to take what he was being offered, but he stood his ground and waited for the right people who understood and respected the role he wanted to play in the development of his product. Wayne considered himself a businessman, not a writer for hire. Ultimately, he was not seduced into taking the lesser deal, and later he met the right folks, who were willing to give him the creative control that he wanted.

Our societal training has taught us to do the logical and safe thing. It has failed to guide us in obeying our intuition. The possibility of making a fool of yourself is always present when you are following your own path and not the one that fits the most common denominator. You will create your own opportunity according to your own criteria to match the unique vibration of your being, not someone else's. In doing so, be circumspect about who can help you and who cannot. Don't jump to conclusions. Be open-minded. Ask a lot of questions. Be bold in asking for what you want. And watch what your body tells you, not just your mind.

You'll get to know opportunity by getting to know yourself. No one's path is perfect and smoothly paved. Even the choices we make from the purest place may contain obstacles, but they are the ones that will teach us what we need to learn to ultimately gain the sustainable prosperity we want. As a roadside sign in India (a friend took a picture of it for me) points out: "The obstacles are not meant to obstruct but rather to instruct."

To Recognize Opportunity

- What do you need to adjust mentally and physically to be more in tune with opportunity? Spend time noticing where in your body you feel fear versus intuition. Notice where excitement might also lead you astray. Do a mental scan of your body when you are making decisions and notice what you feel. Get in touch with your body more overall. It may mean getting back to an exercise regime, moving to music, or doing yoga or whatever feels right to you to awaken your connection to your own body.

- Spend blocks of time devoted to experimenting with how you feel. Feel your way through choices instead of thinking about them. Choose what *feels* right.

- Get rid of things (and maybe people) that clutter your ability to feel and be in touch with yourself. Make space.

- Pay attention to each offer and invitation that comes your way and use your new criteria to decide how to proceed.

- Write down what you already have that can help you reach

your goals and start taking action with what you have.
Don't wait for perfect conditions.

* Revisit the specifics you have listed and record every resource you already have to help you move forward in pursuit of your desires, even if it means asking "dumb" questions
and appearing foolish.

Chapter 4

SECURITY

Life is either a daring adventure or nothing. Security
is mostly a superstition. It does not exist in nature.

—HELEN KELLER

THE desire for prosperity is often rooted in the desire for financial security. It's perfectly normal. We've been very well trained to absorb the need for financial security as a core structure of our lives. This is our rational mind trying to keep us safe, and I will not argue the evidence that financial security is a good thing. Yet here's the big BUT: financial security is an illusion. It can be shattered in a stock market crash, a natural disaster, or an economic downturn. Financial security is an emotional construct. In our world, it is a mental state that depends on our circumstances and surroundings to be true. What I want to challenge is the idea of depending on outside circumstances in order to have security. What if security came from a mind-set that relies solely on itself and not on circumstances? How would the game change if your security did not depend on money?

When I began my business twenty years ago, I had already been an actress and waitress and had survived a nervous breakdown that lasted three years. I had hired a coach two years earlier, before making the commitment to go into business for myself. I began training at the first coaching school anywhere. I had not run a business before except for being entrepreneurial as an actor, often creating my own opportunities when others were not hiring me. I had no corporate work experience; I had never taught or spoken publicly without words from a script; I had never earned more than $36,000 a year; but I had managed to save money, $10,000, which I was willing to live off as I launched a solo practitioner coaching business. I had no prospects and I was in an unproven field. My live-in actor boyfriend at the time, now my husband, was starting a production company with a partner with a few thousand dollars of waitressing cash I had given him. (I kept most of my money in a safety-deposit box because I was afraid to trust anyone with investments and I didn't understand them. What a shame!). By definition, I had no security. However, I had chutzpah, enthusiasm for my product (which had saved my life), and an overwhelming certainty that I could make it. (Yes, skeptics, there was no mortgage or children, but, relatively speaking, the risks were just as real for me as any midlife adult.)

Where did this certainty come from? Maybe it came from standing at death's door and realizing I wasn't ready to stop living. But more accurately, I'd say that I had no other choice. I had already determined that I was not going to die. The career and day job I was in were killing my spirit. Failure at attempting something new was not an option. Failure was not an option. *Failure was not an option.*

Get it? Failure is not an option inasmuch as we can control it. Security comes from that level of determination. We talked about commitment in the last chapter. Here, we have determination and commitment as the first cousins to security. The security that it takes to have prosperity does not come from prosperity itself: it comes from the deepest, most connected part of your core that rockets the message to your mind and engraves on it the ironclad conviction that there will be only a positive outcome. No negotiation. No possibility of missing the mark. This takes tremendous mojo. TREMENDOUS! And that is what it takes.

Every time you doubt, you pull your mind back into the possibility that your dreams may not work out. And what you pay attention to, you will notice more and seem to get more of. So get your attention out of the cesspool of doubt and get it back to creating your prosperity. We can't control every outcome, but we can't expect failure, either. We truly have to reframe failure. If we don't get exactly what we want, maybe we will get something better! Maybe we will get something unexpected that exceeded your own expectations for yourself. This will be your source of financial security: your own determination and lack of negotiation. You are now being fueled by your vision of what's possible for you, not by the cushion of your bank account. Having money as a cushion is fabulous and desirable, but it is not a prerequisite for taking the chances that your desired level of prosperity requires. Let your security come from you, not from any outside circumstance.

How do you do that? It's another one of the muscles that we are trying to build through exercise, through practice. But first, I want to take you to the source of why we often equate money with security.

For most of us, money evokes strong feelings: it brings up emotions from our subconscious and has tremendous meaning in our life stories that keeps it from being neutral. Money is just paper or metal, but it has the potential to move so many aspects of our lives. It is the layers of emotion linked to money that make it so spiritually loaded. When we are able to see money as a commodity, an everyday item, we will have an easier time of transforming our relationship to it.

Money can trigger a variety of mental associations. Think of the emotions that money generates in you. It may be joy or the fear of deprivation. It can bring back memories of great triumph or tremendous suffering. It can remind you of happy times or it can dredge up the anger of being treated unfairly because of how much money you had or did not have. This is what gives money so much power in your life. If you can detach from all that emotion, you can move more freely through gaining and losing money. It's a goal to have as you work through the Prosperity Plan.

Virginia Kravitz, one of the talented coaches affiliated with my coaching company, recently shared a story about a client that illustrates how the emotions of money feed into the illusion of security.

Rose was laid off from a corporate job after a twenty-two-year career, because of downsizing. Though she received a severance package, she was very anxious about finding a job, as she was a single mother with the financial pressures of a high mortgage. She was offered a job in a different department at the same company she had been let go from. She was overqualified for it and the salary was lower than the one in her previous job. She verbally accepted it, although she didn't feel great about it because it felt like a dead end. There would be no room for growth in the role and the thought of it made her spirit droop. But, like many of us, she thought it was better than nothing.

Soon after, another job posting from the same company was published. It was Rose's "dream job," more in line with what she was looking for, with more opportunity to contribute and make a bigger impact. It was also in her dream salary range. The twist was that the timing was such that she would need to decline the first offer in order to interview for the better job. There was a lot of pressure from her family and friends to take the sure thing. Their emotions came into play. It was certainly everyone else's definition of security for her to take the sure thing: "A bird in the hand is worth two in the bush."

Rose was coached by Virginia to go beyond her pros-and-cons list, to stop the noise in her head long enough to hear the "deep truth" about what to do, and to write down what she was *willing* to do. It was suggested that Rose steer clear of all the people in her life who were worried about her and the future of her eleven-year-old daughter. Virginia stressed that no one would judge Rose on whatever she chose to do; rather, the coach's suggestions were intended to help Rose to become clear in her own mind about why she was making the decision she finally settled on.

She decided to go for the new opportunity. She felt emboldened to decline the offer and demonstrate confidence in herself by pursuing what she really wanted. It felt like a courageous move to declare herself worthy of the new potential income level too. Her newfound self-confidence made quite an impression on the hiring manager of the dream job.

The competition for the new position was very intense. There were many candidates and several interviews. Time passed. Rose learned her severance package could be at risk because she had declined a solid job offer. Her fears came lunging back at her, but she was still glad and willing to be taking the risk. Her peace of mind rebounded when she remembered to focus on the deep belief she had in her abilities and goodness.

In the end, Rose was offered the job. It put her into the six-figure salary range she dreamed of being in. She was glad she had held out for the job she wanted. She felt validated that her employer valued her and selected her for it. She had put a stake in the ground with regard to her worth, and had no regret about having made such a public statement of it. There was certainly still emotion connected to her decision, but she had supported the healthier side of it, risk and all.

Like Rose, you need to know what is rock bottom and nonnegotiable for you. For her, it was being able to contribute at her fullest and feeling alive in spirit. Other times it will flat-out be about the money. In creating prosperity, you can declare that you will accept no less than a certain income.

You've probably done something similar to what I am suggesting here with your weight. Maybe you've declared: "No way, no how, will I allow myself to go past X pounds before I start back on a diet!" Maybe you've done something similar in negotiating a business deal. You've known the point at which you'd walk away. No deal, no how.

You need to decide that now with your prosperity quest. Declaring your nonnegotiable breaking point is as important as being specific about the gain you want to make.

Here's a sensitive breaking point that my Prosperity Plan

class participants insisted that I include in this book. Marriage/ partnership and money. So many people expressed deep pain and frustration with the ongoing and often irreconcilable differences between spouses when it comes to finances and talking about money. Emotions run high and the battles can be "bloody." Each partner goes by their own definition of security and the needs and emotions that are its undercurrent.

It is a tall order to separate emotion from money, as I said earlier. When each partner is not there yet, the key becomes dissecting the conflict by realizing it's not really about money: it's about emotion and needs. If the partners could get in touch with what they are really fighting about—and for—the solution would be more attainable.

For example, Janice accepts that her security comes within herself, but her husband clings to money as his security and every conversation about money is intense and confrontational. Janice did not grow up in an opulent lifestyle. Her family did not want for things, but they also did not believe in spending money on designer jeans when cheaper ones did the job. They went on lovely vacations but did not spend a lot on fancy meals or luxurious accommodations in or away from home. Janice doesn't feel strongly attached to her belongings and does not see having money as a reason to have more things, but she does feel free to spend responsibly and use money to enhance their life. Her husband, on the other hand, grew up very poor and clings to every dime he makes. He feels no sense of freedom in his life whether he has money or not. He basically lives with an undercurrent of fear and insecurity. Every conversation he and Janice have about money implodes and makes matters worse.

Janice and her husband, as well as many other couples, need to learn that they are not fighting about money—they are fighting about emotions and needs—and only when they discuss and negotiate the true matter at hand will they have a breakthrough in their relationship and their money life. Each person needs to be clear about what they are really defending or trying to get. Safety? Validation? Freedom? Power? Peace? Comfort?

When Janice could say that money meant freedom to her and her spouse could say that it meant safety to him, they were able to negotiate with more sensitivity and find new ways to handle their money so they could each get their individual needs met as well as start working toward their common financial goals. That's very different from arguing about the shoes Janice purchased or her husband's seemingly stubborn refusal to do repairs to their house. They got to the real issues and got real solutions, but only when they knew how their definitions of security were at odds.

There are yet other battles we fight in the name of security. We sometimes stay in jobs that literally make us sick. We delay making a leap to something we know is our next step for our growth because we are too afraid to give up the "security" of health insurance, a paycheck, and predictability. We stay in relationships that damage us or allow injustices because we are too afraid to become a target ourselves. How can we call that security if we cannot function as the glowing representation of life that we were born to be? What about the high cost of sacrificing our souls? Where do we draw the line?

I have coached many people who have told of getting physically ill and being forced to quit their jobs. Usually these folks who became sick grossly disliked where they worked. One woman was diagnosed as being allergic to the carpeting and plastic furniture; others had medical diagnoses too. I don't dispute those, but I must point out that, in terms of energy, they were not fully able to be their vibrant selves at work. Their bodies actually had to shut down in order for them to survive their choices. It makes sense to me that illness would show up in the body under these circumstances.

One woman quit her job and had to leave her apartment because she could not afford it as long as she was unemployed. She moved back home with her mother and it took her about a year to recover, but she slowly got her energy and her health back. With that came clarity: she found a connection between her former corporate life and her inexplicable love for an old home with a huge porch that was not too far from her mother's house. She wanted to take over the home and turn it into a retreat and conference center for executive meetings. She did just that and has run it successfully for several years. There was never a reoccurrence of her health issues.

I understand where conventional wisdom makes sense. To have abundant savings, investments, insurance, and income does provide freedom and peace of mind. It'll be tough to convince you not to shoot for that, and I am not intimating that you should.

The whole reason for doing this work is to build wealth. But I do want to drive home that no one is truly protected, really. Nature ultimately rules; we don't. So yes, our man-made construct allow us flexibility and resiliency, but it is an illusion. It's not the ultimate bubble that makes you safe from anything life throws your way.

The people I interviewed for this book, most of whom make millions of dollars, all said that security came from knowing they could start over if they had to. Their security did not come from their financial cushions. It came from believing in themselves.

Safety comes from your deep inner knowledge that you can and will find a way to handle whatever comes your way. It's accepting your divinity as a creative, resilient being with a mind that you can use for good. Bless that innate gift of yours and hold it as the core that will guarantee your path to prosperity. That is true security.

To Build Security

- Spend some time writing (rather than just thinking) about creating your own security through your own inner resources.

- Think (and write) about times when your own inner resources got you what you wanted or out of a troubling circumstance.

- Explore (in writing) which of your emotions are triggered by money. What fears come up? What memories? What charge happens in your body and psyche when you talk about money: positive and negative? Learn about your emotional self when it comes to money and notice how you can grow more detached from your emotions and see money as neutral.

- Carefully consider what needs money fills for you. Write down those needs. Realize that your emotional reactions toward money are about those needs.

- Try to get those needs met in other ways if possible.

- If you have a conflict over money with a partner or other people in your life, try to determine what needs and emotions you are fighting about. Learn to get to the bottom of the conflict, because it is not about money per se.

- Record what you are one hundred percent committed to creating and having happen. (Each time you do this, you are refining and tightening as you go.)

* Record your bottom-line, nonnegotiable financial basement, even if it's higher than where you are financially
  now. Write: I refuse to make less than \$_____
  (this month, this year, now, or ever, etc.).
* Write the above statement fifty times, twice a day. (I'm not
  kidding.) As you write, you'll be imprinting this through
  your conscious mind onto your subconscious mind.

Chapter 5

PROSPERITY'S FUEL

Gratitude is the vibration and feeling
that is in harmony with prosperity.

—MARY MANIN MORRISSEY

WHEN you resonate gratitude through your entire being, you calibrate yourself to prosperity. Gratitude is the energy that pulls all other energies toward it and multiplies them. It is the vibration the superconscious thrives on and the one that the "mirror" of the universe reflects back at you in a good way. If there is going to be any emotion around money and prosperity, let this be the one to fuel the journey to what you want to create in your life. It sounds easy, but it is in fact difficult to assimilate gratitude at a core level when there is no evidence yet of your desires coming to fruition.

I remember when I waited on tables in New York City during my years as a musical theater thespian. There was a very difficult old lady who came several times a week to the restaurant for lunch. She was hearty yet diminutive in size. She was strong but not healthy, which was evidenced in the curve of her fingers and the pallor of her skin. She barked orders at the waitstaff in a very abrasive voice as she gasped for air, and I, personally, avoided her at any cost. I did not like this woman, and yet I was not too different from her. I was bitter and angry at that time in my life because I had to wait on customers for a living, when I really wanted to be performing onstage.

One day, it seems it was my turn to deliver the lady's lunch. As I walked the entire length of the restaurant from the kitchen to the very front table where she was seated, I rehearsed how I would not look at her but would try to have the most pleasant look on my face that I could muster. When I got to her table, I gently placed the lunch in front of her, asked her if she needed anything else, then turned to leave, when she beckoned me back to her.

"You catch more flies with honey than vinegar, my dear," she said, wagging her deformed finger at me.

How dare she? I thought as I stormed off, pretending I had not heard her. She was no nicer than I was!

I would not be telling you this story if her wise words had not resonated with me and stayed with me. She taught me something that day, and I hope to pass it on here in a slightly different context. Gratitude is our honey here. We will catch more wealth with gratitude than with worry, fear, anxiety, or vinegary self-torture of any kind.

It's a tall order to find something to be grateful for when you are unhappy with your life or when every story you tell is of woe. It's like tolerating the taste and side effects of an antibiotic when you are feeling miserable. You know you have to take it because it will make you feel better, but the act of doing so is distasteful and adds insult to injury. It's similar with gratitude. The last thing you want to do is be thankful when you don't have enough money to pay the bills or your life circumstances are distasteful to you. So when you ask yourself, "What do I have to be grateful for?" you may be inclined to reply, "Not much"—unless you are actively looking for a salve to help heal and reverse the problem.

I mentioned in the chapter on possibility that the universe acts like a mirror. As a new friend of mine, Eddie Conner, an intuitive, explained it, the universe says *YES!* to you all the time. However, it does it like your reflection in a mirror will. You say into the mirror, "This stinks!" and the universe says: *YES!* And you get more stuff that is rotten. You say into the mirror, "Thank you for the money that is coming in," and the universe says: *YES, money! YES, coming in!* So if you are walking around grousing, complaining, and telling your troublesome tale, the universe says: *YES, here's more to grouse, complain, and spew a tale about!*

It's important to note that this strategy is not foolproof.

One of the downfalls of the recent fascination with this thinking made popular by *The Secret* and many other teachings of its kind is that it's really hard to say that something horrible, like a devastating accident or illness, was the result of something you put out into the universe that was then reflected back to you. There is a school of thought that will tell you that that is so, but *I* won't. Things happen—things that we can't always explain. Furthermore, we cannot account for our own destiny one hundred percent of the time. There are events, good and bad, that shape us in the course of our personal evolution that have nothing to do with what we broadcast to the world.

But that begs the question "Why do this gratitude stuff or intentional thinking work at all?" It *does* work, that's why. It also doesn't hurt. It keeps your energetic vibration up, which is good for your health, your communication, your relationships with loved ones and coworkers, the sharpness of your mind—all of which add up to more prosperity in your life. Gratitude and prosperity are like peanut butter and jelly. They go well together, and who is not grateful for PB&J (allergy sufferers aside)?

Being grateful for what you have sounds like a platitude. Yet we all know it's the right thing to do. It is also how you begin working with what you already have. Does this mean you must accept the status quo and not be willing to pursue what you deeply desire? The answer is no. What diving deep into gratitude does is multiply the energetic vibration of YES in your life. You are recalibrating your whole being to *being* prosperous. You are not saying, "Yes, I am willing to have this less-than-ideal scenario," but you *are* saying, "Yes, this is teaching me something now and I am grateful for whatever it allows toward my goals and desires."

For example, there was a particular time when I had to pay personal bills from my business line of credit. It is not a usual thing for an entrepreneur to do, but it was against my personal rules for myself. I was short on cash. I got angry for being in that position. I felt terribly guilty that I was not contributing to my home in the way I wanted to and I was terrified that borrowing from myself would become a way of life. I had a lot of emotion around money and was not treating it as a commodity. But I reengaged with the principles I am teaching here, turning my pain about lack into something that worked toward prosperity instead of against it: "I am so grateful that I have the means to have this much credit at my disposal," I realized. "I am so grateful for having this line of credit to pay my bills from!"

Within a couple of months of this shift in thinking, my cash flow improved, my need to borrow dissipated, and I was able to start working toward getting my business line of credit back to a zero balance. I am convinced that if I had persisted in my negative, downward mental conversation about this line of credit, it would have become a greater problem.

Gratitude greased the palm of life, so to speak, and I was on to smoother days.

It's not as simplistic as it sounds, either. Just as we shifted our attention from doubts to possibility in the first chapter, the mental shift here is instant, but what you really need to do to change the tide of prosperity is to really feel the gratitude throughout your body in such a way that you really *are* grateful, not just *say* you are. You must truly create a resonance, a vibration, that is conducive to prosperity. That vibration is not bravado, although I know you've seen bravado work for people in your life. The vibration is grace: ease, confidence, focused rapture, and patient expectation. Oh, a tall order. And oooooh, so much fun when you attain it!

This doesn't mean you should just buck up and take what life gives you, even if you are not pleased with it; it means seeing the good in what you have, even if it's not perfect. It's what we teach our children when they receive a gift that is not what they had hoped for. We still say thank you and appreciate the gesture but continue to have our vision of what we truly want.

Keeping the good going, then, means passing the gift on to someplace where it can be loved or used to its fullest.

Gratitude is not just the act of being thankful. Being truly grateful means embodying a gracious attitude. It is grace in action. It's the ability to see what you can be grateful for before your ego kicks in with all the reasons you should be seeing the contrary—and it means allowing that gratitude to morph from a mere brain function to a *whole-body* function. In other words, not just to think it but to *feel* it. In turn, the more you feel it, the more you will think it and eventually start speaking of your gratitude as the truth—truth you whole-heartedly believe and live. When you reach that place, you will be vibrating in harmony with what creates prosperity. Layer that on top of all we've done so far: seeing possibility, directing your efforts into "right livelihood," perceiving and creating opportunity, living with an internal sense of security, and now operating on prosperity's fuel: gratitude. Do you feel the *power?* That is a cellular encoding that is much different from the ball and chain of fear, doubt, worry, lack, and anxiety. In fact, worry is a nudge to be grateful.

There is a paradox here: when you are not prospering the way you want to, it seems counterintuitive to find peace with that. Fear can be a great motivator, after all. When we are panicked, often we take more decisive action. Facing the birth of their first child, many men make strides in their careers. Afraid of losing their jobs, people work harder and behave better. Fear can be a great motivator! However, you do not want to live in the vibration of fear, do you? Being grateful and adopting a gracious attitude while you are in difficult circumstances seems a strange way to behave if you care about changing your financial landscape, does it? And yet, that is exactly what I am asking you to do.

When it comes to money, probably the most insidious manifestation of fear is worry. Worry can run through your mind all day long like an electrical current, sometimes surging and shocking you. It can keep you awake at night in the form of anxiety dreams, restlessness, or insomnia. Anxiety disorders don't even have to be evident before your productivity is cut drastically short, changing your life. Such disorders can become deeply ingrained habits that you may not even notice, because they may seem like merely a quirky personality trait or a lovable neurosis. But do not underestimate the power of worry to snuff out your ability to create prosperity. Just as I told you earlier that the conscious mind cannot always overpower the subconscious mind, worry is an unwelcome inhabitant of your subconscious and acts accordingly. Worry has to be stopped.

Worry and gratitude cannot vibrate at the same time and have positive results. Worry is a lower thought form. It will weigh down the higher thought form of gratitude, which can and should be connecting with the superconscious. They do not belong in the same equation. One must be neutralized and freed from emotion. We do so through gratitude.

I learned the insidiousness of worry at a dinner one night with my friend the Zen master Genpo Roshi, creator of Big Mind process. I'd been a worrier since childhood, but in this meeting I recognized that you can separate worry from money problems.

It was a confusing moment that seemed like a contradiction of truths. Genpo Roshi and I were discussing the downturn in my business at the time and he very purposefully put his hand on mine as it was resting on the table between us and said:

"You never have to worry about money."

Oooookay, I thought. It sounded so auspicious that I did not want to ask him to clarify, but I did wonder what he meant. Was he adopting me? Was he making a psychic prediction?

An hour later I was picking up the check, as I had invited Genpo Roshi to dinner while he was in from out of town, and he asked me if it was really okay if I did that, considering our earlier exchange. I wasn't broke by any means and my husband had a house account, so we knew the check was manageable, despite it being a very upscale place. What I found so confusing was that he was questioning whether I could afford the dinner after he had just told me I never had to worry about money.

But then I got it! Worrying is a choice that is separate and distinct from the money situation I was in. The situation did not require worry. It might warrant it or be justified by it but it did not *require* it, especially if I wanted to correct it. Worry and its relatives—fear, anxiety, panic, and despair—are vibrations that are out of synch with prosperity. Worry is just anxiety about a future that is not here yet. It is wasted energy, and a terrible habit.

Joseph Goldstein, who has contributed to bringing Buddhist teachings to the West, wrote in his book *One Dharma: The Emerging Western Buddhism*: "When we feel true gratitude, whether toward particular people or toward life, *metta* loving-kindness will flow from us naturally." This goes back to our mirror analogy and how we can bring betterment into ourselves by living and giving gratitude. A focus on gratitude takes our awareness and consciousness to its next level of evolution. It strengthens our ability to recognize opportunity, develop security within ourselves, and live in possibility. It is the spiritual currency that will usher in what you are looking for. Gratitude is a much better knee-jerk reaction to life. Develop it.

To Vibrate at the Frequency of Gratitude

- To find your way to gratitude in every situation, practice by writing about an unpleasant time in your life or a "bad" outcome you've experienced. Then record the lessons learned or the people met and their contribution to you as a result of this negative experience.
- Make a master list of everything you are grateful for in your life and visit it twice daily. Start and end your day with it. Drum home the vibration of gratitude by reading this list aloud to yourself.
- Have a gracious attitude with everyone you meet and in every situation you are in.

❀ Practice gratitude as a daily waking meditation. This means paying attention throughout your day to what you can be grateful for despite any appearance to the contrary.

❀ Start the process of being grateful for the outcomes you forecasted in Chapter 1, even if they have not yet come to be. For example, think: *Thank you for the $300,000 I am making this year.*

❀ Change your vibration through all of the above.

Chapter 6

ENERGY ALLOCATION

Life begets life. Energy creates energy.
It is by spending oneself that one becomes rich.

—SARAH BERNHARDT

ON YOUR money journey, you are probably more accustomed to allocating funds to needs or expenses more than you are at allocating your energy. However, that is what this chapter will ask of you. You have been primed by the previous chapters to get here, but now you have to put your game face on. The crux of the Prosperity Plan is to recalibrate your whole being to align with the conditions that invite money, opportunity, and prosperity into your life. Paying attention to where you invest your energy (time, attention, care, discipline, creativity) now becomes what separates those who succeed from those who don't.

This step requires even more courage from you than you

may have demonstrated until this point. It takes courage because you will incur risk. You will need to remove your energy from places, people, and things before you can put more energy toward the good stuff you want to create. You may cause people to become angry with you or you may have to explain yourself when your reasons don't even make sense to you yet, much less anyone else. You will likely have to do things you've put off for quite a long time.

By now it should be clear where you are wasting your time or energy and what you need to begin to do to refocus on creating greater prosperity. As unpopular as this may be, you have to consider that there are people in your life right now who are weighing you down and costing you time, money, energy, and/or emotion. I know that sounds harsh, but these people can be in many different areas of your life: they can be at home or at work; they may be relatives, friends, neighbors, people in your community, your children's teachers or caretakers, the people who assist in your business or work in your home, whether they are doing repairs or help with the day-to-day. They may be at places like restaurants, gas stations, and doctor's offices that you don't feel good about visiting. These may seem like trivialities of daily life, but the truth is you allocate your energetic frequency and life energy to these people or places and you can take that energy back.

Think of your life as a huge, industrial-size tank holding liquid or gas like the kind you might find on the outskirts of a town. This is your life tank. You want your life tank to be full. Now think of all the things that poke holes in your life tank on a day-to-day basis. Who robs you of energy? What situations waste your time? Where are you not contributing your gifts or enjoying your time? Yes, life is full of the mundane, but you will get rid of the mundane as your prosperity grows. Now we are talking about those people and activities that should not even be labeled as merely mundane because they are actually depleting you.

When you reclaim your energy and put it back in your tank, you'll be amazed how much vigor you'll have to create prosperity, and in fact you just may be surprised to see prosperous scenarios start to emerge because you've gotten the deadweight out of your life.

Earlier this year, I pulled the plug on several business relationships that I had allowed to drain me for some time. One in particular was a vendor who had my business for a decade, but in the last couple of years I had been feeling that I was being held hostage, that they had me over a barrel: they did not treat me as a valued customer and knew I was stuck with them or I'd suffer some tough consequences, that taking my business elsewhere would result in a host of other problems that would have to be resolved in order to make the transition. I just did not want the hassle, so I let the drain go on. Maybe you can relate. However, I had had enough, and I had decided to make a conscious effort—just as I'm asking you to do—to take back my energy from the many places where I was letting it languish or even fester into frustration and anger, which is much worse than dealing with the consequences of making a change!

As I expected, the vendor was defensive and threatened that I would be throwing a wrench in my own engine by leaving, but I did not care. It turns out that in the time I had waited, technology got so advanced that I did not suffer the consequences we had all expected and I saved a lot of money in the process.

I can tell you that the result of getting out of four situations that robbed me of energy amounted to tens of thousands of dollars of business showing up within two months of returning my energy (and money saved) to the tank. I do believe they correlated directly.

What you are accomplishing by beginning the process of removing your energy and money from distasteful situations is tackling the very positive task of working with what you have. The money may not be pouring in yet, but you are preparing and making room for it by once again getting rid of the energy drains.

Reducing expenses is part of working with what you have too. One way to "make" more money is to reduce expenses, certainly; but what you are also doing energetically, which you may not realize, is you are creating freedom. When you can exercise choice and free will, you no longer feel stuck. Energetically, you are free. Freedom of movement, a good feeling of being smart and resourceful, and also the life-affirming aspect of exercising choice and free will result. That freedom starts moving positive unseen forces toward you, especially if you have kept your vision clear and your goals focused and you are still living in possibility. That energy is what is encoding your subconscious mind, which is the difference between wishing and making prosperity happen.

It is energy back in your tank when you take control of a situation and find a better solution. Paying less for something and still getting the quality you need is a better energy-producing move than taking no action at all. Oftentimes, cutting back, renegotiating agreements, and unplugging from less-than-ideal scenarios is enough to get prosperity flowing.

There are still other places to retrieve your energy from to refill your tank. You may not have considered what it costs you, energetically speaking, to compare yourself with someone else, if that is something you tend to do. Looking at colleagues, competitors, family members, and even friends and feeling that you come up short is a big energy drain. It puts you in the worry mind-set again. Creating competition, beating yourself up, and using somebody else's measure of success as your own are all mazes with no exit. They will cause you to drain yourself and vibrate fear: the fear of not measuring up, the fear of not "making it," the fear of being "less than" someone else, and/or your own personal brand of fear specific to comparisons you make in your life.

On the other hand, role models are fantastic. If you can keep a positive role model as an example of what's possible without beating yourself up for not being "there" yet, then you've created something to aim for that inspires you. You are moving the example from a negative to a positive, from dissonance to resonance in your body, when you stay focused on what's possible as you compare yourself with someone else as opposed to having that person remind you of what's improbable or unlikely.

David is someone who currently earns seven figures, but he was once making $20,000 a year working on a loading dock. He never graduated from high school, and he looked around and saw plenty of people to compare himself with whom he felt he would never have anything in common with. He grew very bitter and angry as he saw others had choices in their lives while he did not. He had a family to support, and despite working two and a half jobs, six and a half days a week, he felt trapped, with nowhere to turn and plenty of reasons to feel bad about himself. He wanted to go to back to school but did not have the money. He wanted to move his family to a better neighborhood, but he couldn't make that happen.

As he struggled and suffered, David had a mini-breakdown one day while loading a truck. He cried for a moment or two and then heard a voice, almost as clearly as if someone were standing next to him, that said he had to change his attitude. Instead of dismissing the thought, he listened and he wondered how to do that. He thought of his boss, who had a very good attitude. David was able to break down his boss's behavior into things that David himself could do.

David noticed three specific things about his boss. He:

1. loved what he did;
2. did things well and completely;
3. treated everyone around him with respect.

David put his mind to this right away. He began to live the three traits that his boss exhibited. As a result, he got into a conversation with one of the truck drivers who came to the shipping yard where David worked. David would not normally engage with this man, but with his energy in a new place, he did. The driver asked David if he'd ever thought of driving a diesel truck like he did. David said no. He would not want to put himself in harm's way by driving a combustible truck, work such long hours, etc. The driver told David what he could earn in a year driving a truck: $50,000. That was all David needed to hear. It wasn't usually a time of the year that this company hired, but David applied, got a job driving a truck, and was immediately moving from $20K a year to $60K a year, as it turned out, with overtime and other work.

Within three years David and his new energy, which he had put toward good instead of self-pity, comparing, and blaming, were promoted to management in the trucking company. It was a family business, and there was no precedence for anyone who was not family being put in charge. He was even given his own terminal to supervise. Around this time, David had also been making extra money in a network marketing company. He was successful at this on the side. He also put time into improving himself through personal and business development seminars. Eventually, he was a leader in both sides of his career and saw how he could teach others the skills that had helped him succeed. After seven years, going from loading dock to manager of his own terminal, and with a successful side business, David would wake up at night with the clear thought in his head that if he wanted to live his dream of a high income, he had to leave both businesses. He did, and his own entrepreneurial venture is what eventually became a seven-figure business.

For David, it was a matter of allocating his energy through his attitude. He also followed his intuition when it spoke loudly to him. The way he saw himself, his situation, and other people was transformed, and his actions changed accordingly. His own investment of energy was what put the changes in his world into action. It was not luck. It was cause and effect. That is the power of energy. That is the creative force you possess.

Another hindrance to your creative force may be a common mistake that hinders business growth and profits. Having worked with small business owners for many years, I can attest to the fact that many people hold on to customers who are unreasonably demanding and ask for services that are outside of the core business.

Surprisingly, in the name of the prosperity you want to create, even getting rid of clients or customers who give you headaches will do wonders for bringing in good opportunities. I know what you're thinking: *I am following the Prosperity Plan to make MORE money, not lose the money I am already making!* It is no longer right livelihood if you are providing a product or service begrudgingly or just for the money. That is not the way to create the level of prosperity you want. Energetically, it's actually causing you to have less than what you want.

Eliminating the obstacles to opportunity is the key to prosperity, and negatively charged business transactions are one of those obstacles. Because you are eager to make more money, you figure that having a client who is paying is better than having no client at all. Not true. That draining customer is actually standing in the way of your greater prosperity. Garner your courage and transition these folks out of your life. You will be amazed at who shows up in their place.

This isn't just for those in business for themselves, either. It is transferable to any work. Your difficult customer or even coworker will drain you and keep you from giving your best to other customers or your own self-care or your family. Such people will cost you energetically and emotionally elsewhere. They are *emotionally* expensive. Where they will affect your bottom line is that they will be likely to cause you to work for less money because you'll end up working more than you expected to. Furthermore, even if difficult customers are ultimately pleased with their purchases or your services and recommend other customers to you, I guarantee that those new customers will be just as difficult as the ones who sent them. I've seen this time and time again. So, as crazy as it sounds not to take the money when what you want is to make more money, you must also ask yourself if the energy exchange will be equal. Maybe the question you should ask yourself is: *Can I charge enough to make this worthwhile?*

Personally, I have found this question to be a fantastic way to bring more money into my life. I will often quote a prospective customer who is not ideal a hugely outrageous fee. Most times, it will result in them going away, but occasionally they have agreed to the price for the work. It's just fine if they do, because when I am hugely compensated, the energy exchange is evened out and I can do the work gladly. Does that make me mercenary? Willing to do anything for money? No, with my values and my worth uncompromised, the difficulty subsides.

Oddly enough, difficult people behave better when they

have more at stake. I find that, instead of becoming *more* demanding because they are paying me in a big way, these customers usually show more respect for me and the work at hand. What helps the balance of power here is that I am also willing to walk away at any moment. That does not make me uncommitted; it actually makes me *more* committed. If my customer gets in the way of the work, I will remove my energy. Again, this does not make me an inflexible baby. This has made me prosperous. People respect someone who knows their own worth and who won't be intimidated. It is when we are intimidated, fearful of losing the work, or in over our heads (maybe we asked for more than we really felt we were worth and are now in fear mode) that the balance of power is uneven again energetically and drama can ensue.

I was once offered a lot of money to do a work-life balance program for pharmaceutical salespeople. I could tell from the initial conversations that the program was a bit of lip service and not truly meant to change the conditions that caused these employees to be unhappy with their work and life balance. I suggested that we survey the would-be participants about what throws their lives out of balance. Once I presented the data to the hiring customers, I told them that I could not in good conscience do the seminar they wanted from me. I did not believe that their policies supported their salespeople to have a life *at all!*

The company clocked mileage on people's cars and wanted

accounts of every minute of their day. The company not only was dictating goals and benchmarks and sales targets, but was penalizing people if these tasks were not done in the exact way and at the exact time the company thought it should be.

I refused to be a part of a charade by expounding on work–life balance when the powers that be did not truly support such a shift. As a result, they refused to let me walk away and instead took me on for months of additional work, including meeting with the senior sales leaders to hash out what needed to be changed so an adjustment of the salespeople's work–life balance could really be supported internally. Then and only then did we hold the sessions with the sales team that I was originally contracted for.

Energetically, everyone was uplifted. And yet, it was only when I refused to allow myself to be drained by perpetuating a lie or performing a disservice to these hardworking people. And you are doing yourself a disservice when you put your energy where you cannot do your best work, just to get the money. This is not just the dilemma of those in business for themselves. With statistics still showing job satisfaction at less than 50 percent, this goes for those employed by others as well. We block our own prosperity by doing less than the work we love.

It's so simple, really. If you walk around all day hating what you do, resenting people, wishing your time away and probably spewing words to that effect, you are charging your body with negative energy. You are sending out energetic signals like a radio tower, and it is bouncing off the mountains and the prairies and coming back to you as more of the same. More to hate, resent, and spew! The same goes for fear and anxiety: allow those to be the energy you run on and you will be running on it for a long time. Fear gives you more *to* fear. Conversely, if you help the conscious mind and the subconscious mind connect to each other through your awareness and hard work, you can monitor your energy output. Wash everything in gratitude, rebalance your energy equation, and watch your results begin to change.

Allocate your energy within you and with those who you exchange time and place with in the world. Be aware!

To Cause an Energetic Shift

- Observe yourself for a day from an energetic point of view and watch who and what scenarios drain you of energy.
- Make a list of who and what is poking holes in your "life tank."
- Take your energy back from people and places where it is not being used respectfully.
- Reduce expenses more where you can as a way to increase money flow.
- Realize that comparing yourself with others or measuring your success by someone else's standards will only serve to rob you of energy you need to create money with. Take

note of the comparisons that rob you of energy and remind yourself to stop whenever you catch yourself in that line of thinking.

* See if any of the people you compared yourself with negatively can now be positive role models. Add more role models to the list and record what they are doing that you would like to invest your energy into doing as well.

* If you catch yourself putting energy into worrying or fear, pull back and redirect your energy toward what is possible in a positive sense, even if there is no evidence to support those possibilities right now.

* Think about where you may not be valuing yourself enough and how that is draining your moneymaking ability.

Chapter 7

RECONCILIATION

Absence of evidence is not evidence of absence.

—CARL SAGAN

ACCORDING to *Merriam-Webster's* dictionary, to reconcile is to make consistent or congruous, as in reconciling an ideal with reality. And that is what we are going to focus on here. Before we go any further in developing your ability to create great prosperity in your life, we have to stop to make sure everything is aligning, internally and externally. We've set out the big possibility for ourselves, and we've been training our subconscious to catch up with our conscious with the intention of bringing in more money and opportunity. The subconscious is the gateway to what you want to create, and there's more face time needed with that part of you right now.

We have to reconcile that past with the present. As I have

learned from my own personal experience and from the experiences of so many of my clients over the years, a huge holdup to the riches you desire can be past regrets. I have heard so many "woulda, shoulda, coulda's," and I have had my own. It's interesting how embedded those are in people's stories about themselves or, maybe better put, in the identities that they wear. I recently heard a very famous business author and speaker say, in passing and in semicryptic terms, that he passed on a fortune by not staying with a company he was part of in its infancy that is now the number-one entity in its industry. He is famous, rich, and successful in his own right, but he still wears a dunce cap as part of his identity, and admits to it.

I just spoke to someone the day before I sat down to write this chapter who had a crest in his career in show business and now, at a lower point, is WSC-ing ("woulda, shoulda, coulda-ing") himself.

"If I'd only made more of that, I would've . . ."

"I should've known it was going to go away."

"If I'd made a bigger effort to meet more people at that time, I could've . . ."

I understand the very human desire to want to go back and rewrite history. I'd love so much to be able to wave a fairy wand and make it all okay, but it's not within reach to do that in our current evolution and I have no clue if it ever will be. What alternative do we have, then?

Look at the energy of regret. Which category does it put

us in? A vibration of *YES* or a vibration of *NO*? *NO*, obviously. We have to reconcile this, because if we don't, we are putting a stick in the spokes of our bicycle. We have to bring peace to ourselves and forgive ourselves if we want to bring the subconscious and conscious minds into agreement. We need to open the path to forgiveness by realizing we did the best we could with what we knew and had at the time.

Forgiveness is not an easy act to perform, whether we have to forgive ourselves or someone else. I believe that is so because of one core reason. Most people think that forgiving someone, even ourselves, somehow means that we are saying that what was done or what happened was okay. We think that forgiveness means condoning the behavior or action. It is that belief that keeps people from being willing to forgive.

In this case, it's you, and you must forgive anything you are holding over your own head as a form of torture. Whether you gambled away money, made a mistake, took a bad deal, overlooked an opportunity, had a lapse of sanity, or all of the above, you have to realize you did what you could with the level of consciousness and awareness you had at the time. You were who you were and now you are who you are. You have learned. As hard a lesson as it may have been, you have grown from it and are now here, ready to blow the roof off your ability to create wealth. It won't happen unless you help your past catch up to your present by forgiving it—yourself and everyone involved. Here's the bottom-line truth too: You really have no way of knowing if you'd really be any better off if the thing you are berating yourself over had gone the other way. You might have logical evidence that it would have been better, but ultimately there is no way to know. Can you just let it go? Please?!

When you do, a new self-concept will be able to emerge. No longer a dunce or whatever you called yourself, you will be free to have a new, better-fitting one. Like getting a new set of clothes after a big change in your body, you get to start again. This is reconciling your past with your present, but it's also reconciling what you are trying to create for the future with who you are now.

Let's check what you've set out as a possibility for yourself. Does the goal you chose when you started this work really fit you? You may have declared that prosperity, to you, means becoming a millionaire, but maybe your self-concept cannot truly support that. At this point, you need to adjust your specific prosperity goal to something that you really feel comfortable with despite your vision of your wildest dream. It has to fit you for you to be able to create it. Have you reconciled who you are with the person you are trying to create? If you've truly forgiven yourself, you are closer, but is there a block remaining in your thinking or a feeling that could derail your outcome?

The approach here is two-prong. You have to keep eliminating any blocks, but it also may serve you to adjust your prosperity goal. If you can really feel a million dollars (or whatever you are working on) in your body as something you can honestly wear right now as you read this, then keep it. If, on the other hand, it brings up fear or doubt or worry about how you'll do it, lower the goal. It has to fit *now*. You don't have to have a million dollars in your pocket for your prosperity goal to be realistic, but it has to feel exciting and *achievable*, even if you don't know how you'll do it. More desirable yet is to feel the truth of it as if it has already happened and you are already living at that level. If it feels good, keep it; if not, change it to something that feels true right now. To make the connection with your subconscious, it has to be true on a feeling (energetic) level.

The amount of focus needed to maintain this energy and optimism also needs to extend to the whole prosperity journey. Another matter of reconciliation becomes lifting any judgment about the process you are undergoing. I shared that I was a skeptic of this work before it worked for me, and the critical factor that made it work was keeping a consistent level of belief and faith that the outcome I was creating was going to come to be. It is so easy to interrupt your focus and cause hiccups in results by checking your results! If you keep stopping and looking around before your full outcome has come to be, and if you keep questioning whether it will, you will get in the way of the process. It's like kids in the backseat of a car continually asking "Are we there yet? Are we there yet?"

It does not get you where you're going any faster, does it? Just keeping your eyes on the road and focusing on your safe arrival at your destination will move you from point A to point B. And the same goes here. You must reconcile your need for constant feedback and assurance that you are on the right track and just do what is required of you.

If you are tempted to keep repeating to yourself, "It's not working. It's not working," you are telling your subconscious exactly the opposite of what you need to be telling it. It's like sitting in front of a computer, cursing it and tapping a command key with the velocity of a woodpecker hitting a tree with its beak, only to have your computer-genius friend, your child, or a paid geek tell you that the computer only does what you tell it to. You must be doing something wrong! Avoid giving your subconscious directions that lead you to the opposite results of those you most want.

Keep your focus on what you are creating. Be singular in focus. Reconcile what you don't see on the outside yet with what you "see" on the inside, in your mind's eye. The ideal has to be carried like a treasure map imprinted on your being that allows you to be on the quest to your destination. With the determination of an explorer, you must carry on, certain that what you are seeking is out there for the having and not daunted by what life throws in your way.

One of the ways to have this "treasure map" ingrained in your subconscious is to practice visualization. We haven't addressed visualization yet, but it is very, very important to the reprogramming of your subconscious mind to see your outcome in your mind's eye and feel it in your internal life. If you are hell-bent on "seeing is believing," then this is how you will "see."

Using visualization in sports or in healing has proven effective for years. It's a form of rehearsal that programs your brain and body to execute results. It forms a memory in your brain, muscles, and organs that allows a result to be repeated. Again, it's something that takes time, attention, and an investment of energy, and that's why it is not commonplace practice. When I used to be in the theater, I was primarily a singer and an actress but often had to dance. I was good for someone who was not a trained dancer, but unfortunately I did not pick up dance steps under the pressure and circumstances of an audition. However, I did find that when I went home and even thought about the steps before drifting off to sleep, I would always wake up the next day able to execute them without hesitation. I would rehearse in my sleep, programming my brain and body and wake up with "muscle memory." It was like my body learned it overnight and had the memory to reproduce the steps the next day. Too bad that I needed an extra night, but for our purposes that is just fine! That is how visualization works too.

If you close your eyes twice daily and spend five or ten minutes "seeing" the result you are trying to create, you will be using visualization effectively. "See" your home the way you'll have it when you have the money you want in hand. "See" the people you'll be working with, the great influx of customers and money, the people you do well by every day in your new financial status. Imagine the car you'll be driving and the places where you'll drive in it. "See" your children at the schools you want them at and their hobbies you want to support in a greater way. "See" the things you'll be including in your life to make it easier, whether it is hiring help in your home, or getting a service you've been hoping to afford, or taking on another employee for your small business. See what you'll be doing with your money, whether it's spending, investing, donating, or supporting certain people or a cause that matters to you.

When this process began to work for me, I had been visualizing my life as it would be when the amount of money I was working to bring in was achieved. The form it took for me was a mental sweep of the entire property my home sat on. From border to border, I imagined what it would look like once I had taken care of every aspect that I wanted to improve. When I entered my house in my visualization, not only did I see the rooms as I wanted them, but as I mentally entered the room of each of my family members, I visualized what support I would be giving each of them and what skills, talents, and qualities I would be able to help them foster with the additional money. When I walked into my home office in my mind's eye, I visualized the flow of money coming in and out of that space, how many additional people I would hire, and the reach of the work I was doing and wanted to do. This was, and often still is, a daily practice, and it was especially useful if there was any moment that I felt doubts creeping in.

One of my children competes multiple times per year in solo dance competitions. She has worked her way up to the national level of competition. When she started to win consistently, I asked her if she did anything special in her mind to get ready for her contests. She told me that she sees the whole dance in her mind's eye and feels it in her body as she mentally practices.

I also began to see a correlation between when my daughter won and made it to the podium and what she visualized that day. She began winning consistently on days when she announced in the car, en route, that she saw herself on the podium that day. On the days when she reported seeing herself coming in seventh or eighth instead of first or second, I'd ask her if she did not feel right or if something else was up. If not, I encouraged her to see herself as taking first place and then just let it go and have a great time dancing. I have to say that every time she saw herself in first place, she got first place, at least on the statewide level.

"Seeing" your goal allows you to "feel" it, which activates your energetic field and connects you better to the superconscious. If you have to go "back to the drawing board," consider your drawing board to be visualization. If you feel it as true by seeing it in your mind's eye, the self-concept fits, reconciling your ideal with reality. Do not falter. Stay the course!

To Reconcile with Today's Reality

- Put to rest, once and for all, any regrets you have about your behavior around money. Write yourself a letter of forgiveness for any mistakes or actions that you are still angry with yourself or someone else for. Write and meditate on this until you feel no more anger or regret in your body. Let it go.
- Take care to notice, and dig deep if necessary, to discover whether the goal you have set does not really fit your current self-concept.
- Readjust your goal to something you can wear comfortably now.
- Grow the goal as you grow in your self-concept.
- Keep your attention in forward motion. Don't be paralyzed by worry and fear.
- Visualize the desired outcome over and over again until you are comfortable with that picture and really start believing it.

Chapter 8

INTEGRITY

To be persuasive we must be believable; to be believable
we must be credible; to be credible we must be truthful.

—EDWARD R. MURROW

IF a structure has no foundational integrity, it will fall. If your life has no foundational integrity, it will be very, very messy and, likely, dramatic. A strong financial life is certainly part of having a firm foundation to the infrastructure of your life. On your way to shoring up its wholeness, you'll have to tell the truth and face some things you might otherwise avoid. It's not easy to take a good, hard look at yourself and what has brought you to this point, but there is no escaping it. The truth will be your ticket to the other side of your prosperity story.

To help you, I'm going to introduce you to a model like Abraham Maslow's "Hierarchy of Human Needs," which prioritized human motivation. This one was taught to me by my first mentor and teacher in the coaching field, Thomas Leonard. He called it the "I-N-W Model" for "Integrity, Needs, and Wants." This model is used as a model for achievement. I'll explain Leonard's meaning and then add how I use it with clients for financial growth.

In Leonard's achievement model, integrity means wholeness. The major domains in life, like money, relationships, physical environment and health, and well-being, need to be in good condition as a foundational layer of achievement. The second layer involves getting one's emotional and spiritual needs met, like the need to feel safe or free or independent. The third layer is going after what you want and where you can exercise free choice. Life can happen other ways, but as this way suggests, life gets easier and achievement accelerates when integrity comes first, followed by needs and then wants.

Imagine a garden that has been neglected. It's full of weeds, stones, fallen branches; it's overgrown and speckled with moss. You want to divide it into a flower bed and a vegetable garden. Can you do that as it is now? No, you have to return it to wholeness. You'll weed, clean out the stones, clear the debris, turn the soil, and add some fresh dirt. Now the garden is back in a state of integrity. Next, you'll give it what it needs: seed, fertilizer, water, sun, and care. When your flowers bloom, you'll enjoy their beauty and have the choice of what to do with them: cut them, decorate your home with them, press them or dry them, give some away or just let them run their course on their stems. Your vegetables will be there for the picking too. You may eat them, freeze them, preserve them, or gift them. You have choice because you have abundance.

If you restore the integrity of a garden, taking care of its needs, you then have a choice: the freedom to do what you want. That garden is your money life too. It won't grow from a field of debris. It has to be restored to wholeness, and so do you. I'm not talking about perfection but certainly integrity—solid ground or, if nothing else, fertile ground.

What we have here is a bit of a dilemma. Which comes first: making money to get back in integrity or getting back in integrity to make money? It sounds like a catch-22, but it's not. The answer really is: doing a bit of both. To be in integrity about money means being on top of your financial maintenance: balancing your checkbook, knowing what's coming and going, being aware of how much you owe and how your investments are doing. Being in integrity is telling the truth about what is and is not working with your money.

Needs, in the context of money, means using money to cover the absolute necessities before even considering spending on things you want. First, with integrity, you are current, informed, aware, and ready to tackle your money with eyes wide open and the truth being told about your situation.

Once you know what you are dealing with, you budget your money only for your true needs. Then, with consumer debt paid off and regular savings and investing being done, you are really "at choice" and able to design your life for what you want. It's likely you know this already in theory, but you probably do not practice it in reality. You're likely waiting for things to get better on their own.

I know that if you are like many people, the reason you are studying prosperity is to make more money to get out of debt. That's great. But I'd bet my favorite Buddha statue that the elimination of that debt is not your top priority. Your needs and wants are probably running the show.

It is really hard to feel prosperous and to grow financially when you have a lot of debt. Being in debt knocks the integrity of your "foundation." The holes in your foundation need to be permanently fixed by eliminating the debt. According to the survey I mentioned in the introduction to this book, those living paycheck-to-paycheck make up 54 percent of the sampling, and those deeply in debt constituted 15 percent. The hard truth is that a lot of people want to maintain their same level of "wants" or "lifestyle" despite the fact that it causes additional pressure on the foundations of their lives. To be fair, some people find themselves deeply in debt by circumstances that were out of their control. Yet others are entrepreneurs and have to forward money to themselves in order make their businesses happen. Nonetheless, integrity needs to be restored in order to flourish. That doesn't mean that great prosperity can't become yours before you are out of debt, but it does mean you have to be consciously taking care of your money as a demonstration that you can take care of more when it comes. As long as you have a plan to pay it off and don't expect to make it a way of life, you are in integrity. Yes, let's make more money, but let's not use it to increase our life until we eliminate the debt. That is the balance of more money for integrity or more integrity for money. They go hand in hand.

Taking care of the money you already have and having a plan for debt, savings, and giving is making the best of your current situation. We discussed this in the chapter on opportunity. You create a better chance at turning the corner financially when you are aware and informed of your specific money scenario and take responsibility for it with new curiosity and vigor. Most people wait for better times to help them out of their money slump, but part of getting to those better times is creating a strong foundation to leap from.

While returning integrity to your money life is important to creating more of it easily, restoring wholeness to your money doesn't guarantee restoring wholeness to your life. You only have to turn on your TV or read the newspaper to see the next story of a celebrity or sports hero who has gone crazy, trashing a hotel room, getting into a brawl, revealing an addiction, or racking up another divorce to prove that money is not a cure-all. Often people who have great fortunes lose them or what matters most to them in their lives because they are not whole in their mind, body, and spirit. It is not money that makes us whole.

Wholeness in other domains is just as important. To increase your prosperity, you must increase your wholeness. Your health of mind, body, and spirit also needs to prosper as much as possible. This inside-out approach is fundamental to creating prosperity, despite logic telling you otherwise.

Wholeness of MIND

What does it mean to be whole in your mind? Does it require four days a week on an analyst's couch? I don't think so, but it does take whatever practice makes sense to you to bring relative peace to your mind. Ultimately, controlling the small-minded, fearful part of your brain so that it no longer disrupts your life or impedes your ability to create prosperity is the goal. What I mean is that your mind needs to be retrained to see the good, act on the good, and be expansive in its thinking instead of contractive—to be thinking toward growth and life and compassion and love instead of thinking in ways that destroy them.

This does not mean you need to be a saint to be whole. Becoming whole again should make you feel more confident and at peace, not more neurotic because you are trying to be perfect.

Wholeness of BODY

Integrity in your body means taking good care of your body, the vehicle for your soul. Again, this does not mean you have to be a perfect human specimen complete with six-pack abs to be whole of body. It just means you should address what is out of whack in your body and you do your best to maintain good health.

I know this may seem like a lifetime of work in itself, but just know that what is required *now* is that you be in integrity with what you know how to do to take better care of yourself. Again, it's not about being perfect or attaining the ideal, but it does mean keeping your word to yourself. Integrity is about telling the truth. Tell the truth and do what you know how to do. It's a matter of developing the ability to keep your word to yourself instead of being perfect. Just be someone you are proud of, which often means making smaller promises to yourself (and others) so you are more likely to keep them.

Wholeness of SPIRIT

Integrity and wholeness of spirit is rather hard to define. It is the opposite of a broken spirit, clearly. A broken spirit is the loss of hope and the loss of trust in the goodness of life. This trust is a huge component of the Prosperity Plan. It is our spiritual currency. Making one's spirit strong by feeling the connection to a force for goodness is a key element in creating prosperity. I called it the superconscious earlier; it is the source to be tapped to funnel that force into your life. Your own being can be a funnel of reception for that force only if you are strong of spirit. Without a strong spirit, you won't be able to reach for what is yet unseen and unproven in your circumstances.

To mend a broken spirit is to restore one's faith in life. Some do that through religion, others through reading texts that inspire them, through yoga, or by means of some other pursuit that engages the body and the whole being. Still others do so through art or friendship or an exploration of their own making. When we can restore our trust in the goodness of life, we return to a wholeness of spirit and create a springboard for prosperity.

Chloe is someone who has read a few of my books, and life was kind enough to put us together so she could tell me her story of restoring integrity in her life. She grew up on a farm in rural North Carolina where she was taught a strong work ethic and a fundamental Baptist faith. She was always an overachiever who pushed herself through school, college, and law school. After graduation, she landed a job with a prestigious law firm in her area. By all accounts and in the eyes of the family she so wanted to please, Chloe was wildly successful. Her success, however, came at a very high cost.

Working day and night, Chloe shut out her own feelings

to keep what everybody else felt she should have. Despite her body sending her messages of her physical and mental disintegration in the form of a bleeding ulcer and clinical depression, Chloe would not connect with herself long enough to admit that she was not happy doing what she was doing. Eventually, she had no choice but to face the truth about her choices because she had made unwise decisions, using a company credit card for personal purposes. She got caught in a jam, and by the time she came clean with her law firm about her use of the credit card, she was already $14,000 in debt, according to her CPA. However, her law firm's accountant calculated that Chloe had used her company credit card to make $61,000 in unapproved purchases. Chloe pled guilty to a felony and lost her license to practice law. Ironically, many of those charges would have been approved if she had gone through the proper channels and asked in advance. She went from being one of the most respected young lawyers in the area to being an unemployed felon.

Then came the work of restoring wholeness to her mind, body, and spirit. Chloe called her journey the "Chloe Action Plan" (CAP) and took her friends' ribbing with grace. She was asked by a former client to join his business and took a second job at a retail clothing store. She told her story many times as she navigated her new life with a felony on her record, but time after time people chose to trust her.

During her days at the firm, Chloe had ballooned to 351

pounds, but part of her plan was to restore her body. She began exercising and joined Overeaters Anonymous, where she learned a lot about her emotions and why she ate. She went to therapy and began yoga and meditation. She eventually lost 132 pounds and paid off her debt to the law firm plus legal expenses that amounted to hundreds of thousands of dollars.

Reporting to her first probation appointment, Chloe looked around and realized that many of the people in the waiting room did not have the advantages she did in getting her life back in order. As a result, she began volunteering to help people coming out of prison and those trying to overcome their criminal records. She also helped out at women's shelters by sharing her experience.

At one point, Chloe tried to get her law license reinstated. She did not succeed, but in the process she realized she really did not want to practice law again. Becoming a lawyer was something she had done to prove she was worthy. Now she no longer has anything to prove. She's paid off all her debt and bought her own home, which she is calling her "House of Joy." She is back to wholeness and peace, and glad to be discovering what life will bring her next. She credits her recovery to finally understanding who *she* is and what *she* wants.

Once integrity starts being restored, it allows achievement to soar through the satisfaction of needs and then the fulfillment of wants. Restoring integrity allows most of your life dramas to wane and become background noise instead of taking center stage. Integrity involves fixing what is out of alignment with your "right" self, while our last step in reconciliation was about forgiving yourself for those pieces. The mental and emotional clearing first is what will make restoring integrity easier.

What becomes clear when the "hiccups" subside is which needs are motivating you and running your life. We can see from Chloe's story that she needed approval, which she got by pleasing others at her own expense. If it is no longer your messiness or avoidance that is creating problems in your life, you can better decipher what is causing you to make the choices you do. For example, if you have a tremendous need for security or safety, you are going to make certain choices that will affect your ability to live in "possibility."

The question then becomes: Where can you purposefully get the need for safety met without having neurotic or unhealthy behavior around money? Can it come from you? Are there certain relationships or settings that will help quell your need for safety? You want to consciously create ways to meet your needs without having the behavior bleed into how and why you create money flow in your life. When money is intrinsically linked to emotion, as I mentioned earlier, it is difficult for us to be in charge of our financial fate. Money owns us then. We are not free.

Let's say you do have this overwhelming need for safety. It may show up in your life in ways that hold you back by not taking risks (not even calculated ones), hoarding money instead of using it to invest and furthering your ability to make *more* money (through education, investments, business capital, etc.), or being afraid to ask for what you need because being rejected would destroy your safety bubble. These needs must be honored. If not, they will continue to run you. If you honor them, and get them met consciously, *you* will get to own *them* instead of the other way around. The goal is to get them met in ways that serve you and fuel you instead of in ways that throw you back into fear or scarcity.

The needs that control us are as varied as we are, but it is an inquiry worth pursuing. I'll expand a step further with our example of the need for safety by showing you how you might find and name the needs that run your life. I outlined the need for safety above, but it can also show up as a need to worry or as some other kind of behavior in order to feel *safe*. Not that worry itself feels safe, but if we are in the habit of worrying or are prisoners of any other habit, for that matter, the repetition and familiarity of performing that habit can provide safety in itself. We may not like the habit or particularly enjoy it, but its familiarity gives a sense of security and becomes tough to change.

I have been a worrier since childhood and mentioned earlier one distinction I learned about it. There is another one I'd like to share. Worrying about money became a habit I was not even aware that I had. It made me feel safe to worry because it was familiar. Also, I equated worrying with the idea that I was a responsible person. If I did not worry about what I spent, I might become reckless and ruin myself financially, you see? It was very difficult to dismantle that habit and understand why I was worrying, even when I had plenty of money, because I had somehow created the mental construct that I was responsible and therefore good *because* I worried. Now that I'm distanced from it, I see that worrying not only made me feel safe and responsible but prevented me from truly prospering joyfully and therefore more fully.

The first step to rectifying this situation is to be aware of it and how it affects you; the second step is to cease the behavior; and the third step is to recalibrate your body through gratitude and some of the other qualities we've been studying in order to connect your consciousness to the flow of life (the superconscious) and eliminate the drag of our subconscious mind.

Getting your needs met in healthy ways allows you to be free to live your wants. You can spend money within reason on things that enhance your life; you can use your money to further causes for the betterment of others; and you can have freedom and choices! Our needs run us to the point where we don't even realize that we can actually feed those needs and get them off our back. Such needs are so deeply ingrained and so insidious that we treasure them as a personality quirks instead of seeing them as unmet desires, probably dating back to childhood, that can be set aside in order to put our whole mind, body, and spirit back in alignment.

Therefore, managing your needs will allow you to satisfy your wants. Those people who are truly free to be rich are so because they expect it; they don't fear it, they don't feel guilty about it, and they experience the world as a generous and giving place. As you well know by now, you can and will have this experience when you see it as true for you. Those who beat the odds don't even think about doing so. It doesn't occur to them. They see it as their right to expect wealth. They see it as an essential buttress of their structural integrity and know they deserve it.

To Restore Integrity, Honor Your Needs, Live Your Wants

* Restore your integrity with money by visiting with your money. Balance your checkbook, reconcile your statements, file your paperwork, know what you owe, and devise a simple payment plan to get back on top of it. Study your statements and see how your investments are doing. Start up an automatic investment or savings plan, no matter how small, if you haven't already. I know I make it sound easy. It is. Put thirty minutes a day into it until you have a system in place. Once you do and you keep it up monthly, it is not that hard.

* Ask for help to do the above, if needed. There is nothing to be ashamed of. There are many, many books to help

you do this: See "Resources" at the back of this book.
Again, thirty minutes a day. You can do it.

* Shore up your infrastructure mentally, physically, and
spiritually—and your chances of achieving your prosperity
as a result.

* Take courageous steps to tell the truth.

* Write down what drives you. What needs are not being
met in your life that show up in your behavior and attitudes
toward money? (For example, the need for safety, security,
luxury, a short-term high, control, ego satisfaction, keeping up appearances.)

* What would it mean to live a life of your wants? Write
down what that would look like—the life of your wants.
How does it match your list of what's possible?

Chapter 9

TIME AND TRUE MOTIVATION

*The only reason for time is so that
everything won't happen at once.*

—ALBERT EINSTEIN

TIME is an unpredictable factor in the Prosperity Plan. Most people will be looking for a quick way of creating an in-flow of cash. Results can happen quite fast and unexpectedly, but often only after some serious effort to recalibrate how you do things. Unfortunately, bank-filling tender is not always as timely as we'd like, especially if we have a lot of mental retraining to do. It's frustrating and probably not what you want to hear. Remain in action and do not judge this process. It's so easy to say "It's not working" and go back to your old habits.

I've been there. I did that myself, but fortunately for me, my mentor would not let me off the hook, so I stayed with it and saw results. I understand the temptation to quit when the things you want don't come quickly. But consider this: What could be harmful about retraining your mind consistently to see and bring you opportunity and money? Why would you give up, even if the results aren't coming as fast as you'd like? It's like giving up exercising because you did not lose as many pounds as you wanted as fast as you would have liked. Will you lose more by quitting? I'm certain that you feel better after reading this much if you've been answering the questions and adopting the suggestions than you would if you hadn't.

Do not make an agreement with failure. Do not give in to the weight of your subconscious programming or your inner doubter.

At one point, when I got frustrated trying to relearn the mental habits that I had unwittingly succeeded with when growing my income in my early thirties, I decided to try an experiment. I was feeling sleepy and was about to take a treasured afternoon nap. That is my favorite time to visualize something I am working on and see it materialize and break through the inertia of the subconscious. I told myself repeatedly as I went off to sleep that I would bring in $3,000 in the next forty-eight hours. (I purposely tried a relatively low number because it was not much of a stretch.) When I woke up within the hour, the first e-mail I read upon getting back to my desk was that I had just secured a small engagement for $3,000. That was FAST! You may call it a coincidence, but I saw it as a confidence booster and a step in the right direction. It was enough for the skeptic in me to wither, allowing the student to become a believer!

One common quandary that I've heard many clients mention over the years involves how to know when it's time to quit. How do you know if you are supposed to keep going if your dream doesn't seem to be working out?

It's never worth giving up the dream to better your life financially. It may change form in terms of how the money will be earned or where it will come from, but giving up on a better life is not an option.

It's so easy to get discouraged or to interpret a lack of results as a failure. When I was an actor, my lack of extraordinary results made me interpret my entire career—and my life—as a failure. I fell into such a deep depression because of that belief that I considered ending my life. However, I can tell you today that nothing about my life as an actor was a failure. It serves me so well today as a speaker or when I have to be on TV or emcee an event. It's a pleasure to have performance skills and must have been part of some grand plan, because they continue to benefit me despite my having given up performing as a career.

Seth Godin, the author of *The Dip: A Little Book That Teaches You When to Quit (and When to Stick)*, is my favorite source when it comes to deciding whether to give up on a dream. In essence, his book says that the way to know if it's time to quit on a business is if you no longer have it in you to be the best at what you do. If you no longer want it badly enough to commit to be the best at it, then it is time to quit.

I'd add that if you have fallen out of love with what you are up to, you may have outgrown it or evolved past it. It would be time to chart a new course.

One easy way to know if you are willing to challenge yourself to beat the odds is to ask yourself what you would have to give up to get there. Is it worth it to you? Are you willing to do—and give up—whatever it takes to get what you want? I know of many people who pine over goals that have not come to be but, when pressed to answer these questions, have to admit that they are not really willing to make the sacrifices needed. So no wonder they are not manifesting what they want!

In addressing time on the prosperity continuum, I'll tell you the story of two friends of mine, a male/female business team who had a financial increase goal in mind and decided to read and do all the exercises in *Think and Grow Rich*, Napoleon Hill's famous book. They spent thirteen weeks reading every chapter and following every suggestion it gave. When they were done, they had no financial increase to speak of. Where most people might have thrown the book across the room, cursing its very existence, they decided to continue the practices they had learned in the book, as you will do with the practices here. Within three months of officially ending the work in the book, they landed a book deal that brought each of them the exact amount of money they had made their focus when they started the journey. Needless to say, they both keep up the practices they have learned from the Hill book and their lives have continued to remain on the increase in terms of money, scope, and reach.

Time speeds up once results start happening. Suddenly, seemingly out of nowhere (despite hours and hours of visualizing, taking action, and retraining your mind!), you will unexpectedly get a check. Or perhaps a wonderful money-making opportunity will come to you with no apparent effort. It may seem like no effort, because in our old success thinking you may have expected to consult your network, meet with the most influential people you knew, or make three hundred phone calls to get such positive results. However, in our new paradigm, you changed your subconscious receiver and transmitter and the signal was picked up and results materialized. Yes, you took action, but you added new tactics in alignment with your new understanding of what you are capable of as a human being.

One of the folks in my Prosperity Plan classes recently told me that she realized she needed to carry more cash in her wallet because she was always opening it and telling her two sons that she did not have any money. It dawned on her that this was not true, but she kept repeating it to herself and sending a very strong message to herself and to her boys (and the "mirror of the universe"). As soon as it occurred to her, she kept more cash on hand, stopped repeating her baseless mantra, and within less than a week received an unexpected check for $100.

Everything we've looked at so far is encapsulated in that example. This person removed an energy drain, changed her language, and corrected what she was projecting into "the mirror of the universe." She stopped transmitting *I have no money* and began taking into her subconscious the mental picture of money in her wallet every time she opened it and more money showed up. That sounds so easy, and yet it really *can* be that easy.

On the other hand, time seems to stand still when we doubt, worry, and get angry that we are not getting what we want. It causes us to curl back up into our cocoons and return to our old mental habits. Think of how long you have been in fear mode or angry about your circumstances. Think of how you bitch and moan and what most of your thoughts or spoken words include. Do you tell everyone you know about your problems or maybe hold them in out of shame until the pressure causes you to explode with sadness or rage? By doing either one, you are only cementing patterns that will keep you exactly where you are. Time feels endless when we are in that state. So, what is the answer? Avoid activating the frequency of disappointment in your body. Keep practicing everything we have done so far and spur yourself on with a healthy motivation.

To create prosperity in your life through a recalibration of your thinking and actions, you need to consider the energy and intention with which you'll be producing your results. We want high-vibration intent and power behind your quest for wealth. What will you give for this wealth? How will it pay forward? How will your increase contribute to the whole? The more your true motivation is positioned in a life-enhancing way, the greater the energy behind your quest for riches.

I know you've seen many examples of people who make a lot of money without caring one iota about others or how their money will be of service to society as they progress. Obviously, higher-level thinking isn't always a prerequisite for creating wealth in your life. However, if you were like that, you'd be doing that already; and since you are not, this is the way for the folks who have a heart. Your desire has to be intense, but you don't have to be aggressive or burn bridges while you make your way.

That is not to say that the whole desire behind wealth has to be for altruistic causes. However, it does mean revisiting "oneness" and connectivity in order to tap the life-giving flow of prosperity that is possible when one's true motivation is aligned with the greater good. As our world shifts from competition to collaboration, recognizing the connectedness of all things becomes not only a way to serve the world with your gifts but also an idea that allows you to tap into the universal energy that is available to us all.

What is your motivation for more money? What will you do for it? What will you do *with* it? Who will you support? How will you be a greater contributor in the world because of it? Remember, with your needs met, you can live from your wants. How will your money—present and future—help increase life for everyone around you? This is a shift from being a consumer and a spender to being a "creator." You create money. You create opportunity with your money. If you are part of a company, you may even be creating jobs.

It is nature's way to grow. All life grows with no thought, worry, or guilt. When we want to increase our scope in terms of riches or a job or a family or an enterprise, we are merely bending to our innermost instinct to grow. It is encoded in our DNA to do so. It has nothing to do with our ego.

In wanting more for yourself and increasing your self-concept, you increase what you are willing to allow into your life and what you are willing to ask for. Once you receive it, you can continue to grow and become a "creator." The *essence* of you increases. You increase your scope and you enlarge the space for those you touch through opportunity and support.

The word *creator* might make you uncomfortable because it is often reserved to describe God. Let's say you are tapping into the goodness out there that is God-like. It's okay. It's there for you. It's nothing to shrink away from. Someone who makes more for everyone as they increase for themselves is powerful. Have no fear of it.

In my work on this, I stated that I was willing to do great work for great pay with people I share great energy with. I was clear that my work was about raising consciousness on the planet. Specifically, I also was willing to eliminate any debt with my increase. I wanted the increase to help support my children's dreams and desires, which at the time meant national dance competitions for my daughter, a budding professional career for another, and learning resources for a third. I also very much wanted to donate a lot more money to organizations that interested me and did great work in the world. This was another reason I knew that my energy and positivity as someone who was making this increase occur was also a positive contribution to the world around me.

It is important to have the "why." It keeps you going and it feeds into the universal mind-set that wants you to succeed. The hardest part is *our* part: being patient and having trust in the goodness of life.

Paciencia y fe is Spanish for "patience and faith." It also happens to be a song title from the 2008 Tony Award–winning musical *In the Heights*. The song has a payoff in the plot of the show, which I'll share with you, but it speaks to the writer's story as well.

In the Heights began as a project the writer and director, Lin-Manuel Miranda, wrote during his sophomore year at Wesleyan University. In the winter of 1999 he applied to put up a new show in the student-run '92 Theater. At the time he had one song written and a title. When they said yes, he wrote instead of eating or sleeping. He wrote a deeply personal show that mirrored how he had grown up in the Latino neighborhood of Washington Heights in New York City.

Miranda's show, with its inspiring message, broke box-office records for the '92 Theater that year. John Buffalo Mailer (son of writer Norman Mailer), who was a senior at Wesleyan at the time, also saw it. He loved the show and said to Miranda, "My friends and I are starting a production company when we graduate and we want to help you bring your show to New York." The author loved hearing the offer, but forgot about it almost as soon as he heard it. It was one of those "Wouldn't it be nice . . . ?" encounters as far as the writer was concerned.

A couple of years later, Miranda ran into director Tommy Kail in the basement of the Drama Book Shop in Manhattan. It turned out that John Buffalo Mailer, Kail, and some other folks had in fact founded a production company: Back House Productions. In that encounter, Miranda recalls, Kail explained what he liked about *In the Heights*—as well as what he would do if he were its director. Miranda says that he was struck by two thoughts: "This guy is smarter and understands the show better than anyone I've ever met," and "Crap. I have to completely rewrite this show."

Over the course of the next year, Back House Productions staged *In the Heights*—still a work in progress—several times while Miranda worked at his old high school, where he taught English to seventh graders. Producer Jill Furman came to a reading and joined the production team. *Rent* producer Kevin McCollum came to a reading and got his production partner interested as well. The show went from Off-Broadway to Broadway and won multiple Tony Awards in 2008.

The song "Paciencia y Fe" that I mentioned earlier is sung in the show by the hero's adopted grandmother. She sings of her dream to get back to her country, which she supports by playing her lottery tickets faithfully. She knows that one way or another, lottery or not, her dream will come true. She does end up winning a big jackpot, only to pass away and leave it behind to the story's hero, originally played by Lin-Manuel Miranda. As the play comes to a close, he tells us he is taking the winnings and moving back to the Dominican Republic to fulfill his dream of having a business on the beach.

What I hope is illustrated by both these stories—the real and the fictitious one—is that money doesn't come from money or your deep knowledge of how it works. Money comes from an idea. An idea that you love so wholeheartedly that it moves you to do great things. It moves you to focus, to labor, to work with so much joy you don't even know you are working. It moves you to be patient, because you know it's just a matter of time.

What is your *idea*? Is it a big wish you have for mankind? Is it a product? Do you fill a need in the marketplace with a service? Is it a way of being and participating in the world that fuels the goodness of life? Is it an innovation in your job that you are willing to champion? Is it the idea of how you can live your life that you never felt was possible before?

As long as the idea fuels you, it does not matter if the idea is the business you want to create, the job you want to get, the people you'll be serving with your money, or the lifestyle you want to lead. The BIG IDEA does not guarantee the absence of failure, but any setback is not a dream killer. It becomes a lesson on how to get one step closer to the dream even if you have to allow it to change form as you progress.

To Tap Your True Motivation

- Have a sit-down with yourself about patience and faith. What do you have to do to develop that muscle?
- Write down the assumptions you have about time that come into play in your prosperity plan.

* Write down why you want to create the prosperity you crave. What will you do with it? How will you become a "creator"?

* What is the idea you are in love with that fuels your prosperity journey?

* Is your BIG IDEA the goal you set out to achieve here originally? Is it the outcome of winning that goal? Is it something you still want to create? What is the BIG IDEA?

Chapter 10

YOU BEING YOU: IT'S ENOUGH TO MAKE YOU PROSPER

Let the world know you as you are, not as
you think you should be, because sooner or later,
if you are posing, you will forget the pose,
and then where are you?

—FANNY BRICE,
vaudeville performer and Ziegfeld Follies star

∞

BEATING the odds and creating extraordinary wealth and happiness from now on are directly connected to the unshakable knowing of what you are about. Yes, despite your shortcomings, puckers, bad moods, and lack of know-how, you can "make it" on just being YOU.

Every client success I've ever shared in came about because of the process of telling the truth about who these people were and what they wanted. The difference lay in people's allowing it to be told, honored, held, acted upon, and even energetically insisted upon. This doesn't mean you'll get by on your good looks alone. Effort is required, but the effort that is needed is clear when you have done everything this book has asked you to do until this point. If you've done all of it, you are poised to be yourself more freely and, therefore, be more of a magnet for opportunity and money.

Each part of this process has allowed you to tell the truth about what you really want and what you know deep down you are capable of. What you have done is drill down to a clarity that has allowed you to find YOU again. You need to deeply assimilate that being YOU is enough to bring in great prosperity. It's not your list of what you're not or hope to be someday that will bring you money and opportunity. It's knowing WHO you are, WHAT you want, and WHY you want it that is the rocket fuel in your life tank.

Look at the letters in the word *you*. Y-O-U. Your Own Uniqueness. That says it. It's enough to be your own uniqueness and allow it to stand out as your brand and your reason to succeed. There is only one Wayne, one Lin-Manuel Miranda, one Ali, one David, one President Obama, one Bill Gates. Their uniqueness made their stories and their success, not the other way around. They trusted their guts and lived with conviction about the idea they loved enough to make it their reason and path to prosperity. Their uniqueness had to bump up against other people's uniqueness at some point in order to be made whole, moving their idea to fruition and success. That's where accepting what you are not becomes just as important as knowing who you are. These success stories included understanding where help was needed, where they didn't need to have all the answers, and where creating a group around them that might be smarter than they were was a good thing.

I was recently working with a young CEO who runs a midsize business in New England. As his company grew, he felt more and more pressure to become a different kind of CEO than he had been up until that point. He felt he needed many qualities he did not already possess and that he was missing some expertise. He grew increasingly anxious as he more tightly defined what a CEO should be by outside standards and expectations. When we finally got back to his UNIQUENESS, we saw that there were certainly strengths that he had that benefited his company greatly. He had a choice: he could get someone else to become the CEO he was not, or he could remain the CEO, accepting the strengths he had and being sure to delegate the parts that were not his to own. It took some tough swallowing but he eventually saw that being himself brought many good assets to the company that it could benefit from and that he did not have to be like anyone else to succeed. He could be himself *and* lead the company *and* delegate the pieces he did not want to do. His company's profits began to increase once he stopped hiding behind his doubts and fears, accepted himself for what he could do, and got the rest of his organization into action. He could not perform at peak and, therefore, could not lead well when he was still questioning his abilities. Once he knew what he *could* do, the pieces fell into place and the money kept coming.

A big mistake that people make is investing energy in prerequisites. The assumption is that we have to know something additional, have another credential, be or look a certain way, have specific experience in something, or otherwise put a great contingency on our share of the prosperity pie. What do you say has to happen in order for you to make more money? The truth is you don't have to be anyone different from the person you are right now to prosper. The only prerequisite to start seeing more financial abundance in your life is to remove the noes to being you. Working with what you have, which I've been saying from the start of this book, means just being more of you. Not a different you—not a taller, better-looking, smarter, more educated, or more experienced you. Just YOU.

It's time to remove, undo, and dismiss all the blocks to YOU. What are your blocks? What you can or cannot do, what your parents did to you, the injustices you have suffered? What you look like, sound like, smell like? Any mental projections you have created are just lies about who you are and need to go. There is nothing to add; just subtract everything that detracts from you being YOU.

I've been working with a young doctor in Europe who was struggling to move her new career in a direction that would give her what she wanted. She lost months to depression, confusion, and anxiety before she called me to work on a career direction. She wrestled with setting herself up for fame and prestige as a doctor. Which path would give her that? Research? Surgery? Coming to America?

She had jumped ahead in an attempt to control an outcome that had no "why" behind it, other than to start making money and get on a professional path. She wanted to be ten years into her career now with accolades and guarantees of wealth in hand. Positive thinking and all considered, that was not possible without a time machine!

She had lost her way by thinking she had to be more than she was at that moment. As is customary for me when clients are out of touch with themselves, I asked our young doctor to take on a hobby or distraction that put her back in touch with her senses. I usually assign something that involves using one's hands, like painting, clay molding, gardening, or knitting. When she came to our next call, she told me she took to practicing her suturing on a raw chicken! She reported how she cried with joy as she got back to working with her hands and the skills she had learned as a doctor. She instantly knew that she just needed to get herself a position practicing her art, performing the work she loved. She did so within a couple of short weeks. She got a position in a good hospital, she was doing what she loved, and she knew that her path would unfold as it was supposed to with awareness and wise decisions.

She just had to get back to being herself and the answers would become clear and the opportunities immediate. She respected herself enough to finally get back to what she loved. Not to mention, she went from being broke and borrowing money from her parents to being gainfully employed and decently paid just by reaffirming the truth of who she is and what she wants. Just two months into the job, she was being offered more lucrative positions at other, more prestigious, hospitals.

On the most essential level, we are all LOVE. Yes, you read that correctly: love. The energy of life, the deepest need, the most essential source of all that is good. The energy that can create and that can move the most stubborn; the substance that nourishes life. Love brings you back to yourself. Love brings you to what is right about you—your divinity, if you will.

Oprah Winfrey, one of the richest women in America, speaks openly about seeing herself as a child of God. (That certainly affirms her belief in her own divinity!) Despite the flaws and struggles she has so publicly shared with an international audience, her self-concept as a being of divine nature and living in service to that same nature in others has helped her tap into extraordinary wealth through her varied media.

What we can borrow from this example is a model for living in the energy and vibration (our spiritual currency) that will change your circumstances. Is it just that Oprah has a connection to the flow of wealth from the universe that the rest of us can't access? If she is a child of God, is she the favorite and we are forgotten? No. We all have the capacity to love ourselves and transform our situations into an energy that can produce the outcomes we want.

At the outset of this book, I quoted John Naisbitt, who said that the true discovery of the twenty-first century will be the understanding of what is truly our capacity as human beings. Perhaps that is our capacity to create something from nothing. To connect to others, ideas, resources, wealth, and prosperity without the expected prerequisites, such as status, connections, education, breeding, a good résumé, and all the other things we have agreed to in society and five-sensory, conventional living.

Our capacity as human beings that is emerging into our consciousness for our own evolution is multifaceted. We are understanding more about our brain and how it works, quantum physics, our ability to heal ourselves and one another, and how to create new ideas. We are slowly turning our faces to the light of understanding that we are capable of much more than what we have come to resign ourselves to being in everyday life. Our capacity to create in new ways is being called on especially right now. We are being forced to create work for ourselves in untested water. We are being challenged to reinvent business, health care, religions, growing and distributing food, caring for the planet, and every domain of human life. This aspect of our capacity is being called upon to make straight all the crooked places in our world right now.

Your human evolution includes understanding that you have the innate ability to tap into all the goodness (love, wealth, prosperity, health) available for the taking. Goodness is a renewable, sustainable resource if we keep ourselves attuned to the vibration and energy level that invites and keeps it.

Does bad stuff happen? Does the negative subconscious win out sometimes? Do tragedies occur? Yes. And that still does not change the fact that we can start again and re-tap those unseen resources for strength and solutions. It's about not allowing anything to diminish the divinity in you. There is no prerequisite to your prosperity other than believing that it can be yours.

YOU *Revealed*

* Examine where you still have blocks to being YOU. What excuses do you hear yourself use about why you can't make more money or execute the plan you are working on. Write them down and state in writing what you'll do about it.

* Write down what resistance, if any, comes up for you when considering yourself as LOVE or a divine being. What keeps you from embracing that? The language? The image? The implied presence of God or a higher order?

* Write down what other structure could work for you to embrace the superconscious (universal) mind.

* Write down how to best champion the goodness in you and in your surroundings. Spend more time doing that.

* Keep practicing your visualization twice a day and layer on the possibility that things can be effortless in your life. Action is needed, but being in the energy of what you are trying to create is just as important as the actual legwork that you will do.

* Make note of where you are now. What have you created? What signs do you notice of things turning your way?

THE PROSPERITY PLAN

Change is not a destination,
just as hope is not a strategy.

—RUDY GIULIANI,
former mayor of New York City

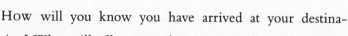

How will you know you have arrived at your destination? What will tell you are there? How will you feel? Who will you be?

By now, you should feel different. You should be seeing some things changing. You may have already grown money as a result of shaking the bushes and rattling up your world. But the work is not over. It can take one to five years to build a sustainable business, eight months to three years to dig out of debt, and at least a year in a new job to start hearing about future possibilities. So what do you do in the meanwhile? You work the plan. Relentlessly and with gusto. You also keep the mind-set as a permanent life change. As the Weight Watchers people say: "This is not a diet. It's a lifestyle." This is not a onetime course. It's a refreshing way to live!

Prosperity consciousness is a way of being, and I hope you never lose your way from it again. It is developing your personality as a "creator." Everything you touch may not turn to gold, but it will be better for having been touched by you. People, places, things, and ideas are better because of you. That is prosperity "beingness." A walking example of the consciousness. As you know by now, *this* more than anything will help pave your way to more money. Before now, you knew how to have more wealth—spend less, make more, live within your means, reduce debt, save more—but what will make the difference? What will make you act on this knowledge? Your consciousness. Your belief that you *can* do these things. The belief that these things will actually make a difference. *That* is the work you've been doing, and it is the work that must never end.

It is from here that you are ready to soar with your dreams. You may be the type to read a book first and then go back and do the exercises. If so, start now. If you've been doing the exercises until now, it is time to review, tighten up your planning, and use this final section to set yourself up with a point of reference to visit at least twice a day to be sure you are executing your plan.

People tend to ignore the small successes along the way,

but now is the time to take stock and realize you have already started to create the results you want. Once you start the momentum going, the positive results can be multiplied. This is also the time to tighten the specifics. What are you creating? What steps will you take to create it? Things may take on a life of their own, and plans can change. The flow of goodness is likely to take over, but in the meantime you can't take action on generalities, so you must have specifics to move.

Manifesting money or something you need may sound magical. Maybe it is, but I see it more as programming. Programming yourself to know you have the power to create what you need; programming yourself to recognize the opportunity to ask for what you need or perhaps demand it; and programming yourself to be consistent in thought and action until the results take form. Manifesting results is harnessing your thought to create something from nothing. It takes seeing, believing, asking, tinkering, taking action, intensifying your desire, and sometimes getting mad enough to recommit time after time, after time to creating what you want.

The same goes for what you are doing here. If you are not willing to do what it takes (and eighty percent of people are not), then go back to your old ways. You need to push through the hiccups and keep going. Recommit every day that you are going to succeed at what you have set out to do. Remember, there is no room for doubt.

The Idea I LOVE!

What's possible?

I can:

I will:

I have:

What I envision:

What I already have to start with:

What I am grateful for:

To Be Made Right
(things I need to forgive, reconcile)

Restoring Integrity *(what I have to fix in my life and finances)*

Energy Allocation

Give to:

Remove from:

Timing
By when would I like my idea to come to be

Who I am that makes this possible

Now do!
Actions I commit to take for the idea I love

Hope recently moved next door to Courage and the two of them shared a conversation about you in the hallway. Hope wanted to tell you to keep her in your heart and if Doubt shows up, tell her you're not interested. Sometimes Doubt shows up without an invitation, so be ready!

Courage had a few words for you as well. Courage wanted to remind you that sometimes Fear's long shadow lurks in the corner, waiting for the unexpected. He will try to tell you stories and make you feel afraid. Speak out boldly and keep Courage by your side. Look Fear in the eye and refuse to follow him. Don't give up. Don't you ever give up. Then Fear will never bother you again.

Keep us, Hope and Courage, close to your heart. We will be with you when you need us most and help drive out Fear, Uncertainty, Pain, and Doubt.

—*Pascale Eenkema van Dijk, twelve-year-old daughter
of a Prosperity Plan class participant*

ACKNOWLEDGMENTS

This book was written thanks to the interest and dedication of Joel Fotinos, my publisher at Tarcher. A teleclass offering on my website caught Joel's eye, and the next thing I knew, I was writing a book about it. Thank you, Joel, for your friendship, humor, vision, and undying support.

Sara Carder, editor extraordinaire, thank you for jumping into this project with the same enthusiasm and care you always have for what I do. I appreciate your point of view, your honesty, and your open-mindedness.

To the amazing team at Tarcher/Penguin, from sales to publicity to production—thank you so very much. Andrew Yackira and Brianna Yamashita, a special extra thanks. David Chesanow, who copyedited this book, I thank you for your meticulous care.

I am grateful for the support of my agent, David Hale Smith, and his amazing assistant, Shauyi Tai. I appreciate your valiant efforts to follow my erratic path. Your enthusiasm for the journey makes it all the more fun.

Thank you to all the people who allowed me to interview

them for this book. Some have chosen to remain anonymous, and the rest are mentioned by name in the book. I appreciate your candor and the privilege of sharing your stories. To the participants in my Prosperity Plan classes, thank you for your feedback and support, and for allowing me to learn alongside you. An extra spoonful of thanks to Virginia Kravitz and Joanna Fabrizio for holding down other parts of my business while I wrote this book, and a debt of gratitude to Christina von Fengler (formerly Jancsik), my assistant, who fulfills more functions on a daily basis than one person can count! Thank you for being such a champion of me and my family. I depend on you so! Thank you for that.

I humbly acknowledge my stunning mentor and friend Mary Manin Morrissey, who has patiently guided my prosperity studies and turned around so many murky corners of my thinking. I would not have been teaching and writing on this topic if it weren't for you. Thanks for your generosity and for sharing your gorgeous, luminous spirit with me.

To my amazing husband, Mark, thank you for taking every book ride with me with such patience, humor, and enthusiasm, not to mention all the entertaining of our children and juggling you do when I lock myself away to hear my thoughts and write. And to those delicious children—a nod of thanks for being interested in my work. I love you all. I am so grateful that a writer's life allows so much time with you.

RESOURCES

These resources were chosen for their accessible, easy-to-understand instruction:

Jean Chatzky

The Difference: How Anyone Can Prosper in Even the Toughest Times. New York: Three Rivers, 2010.

Make Money, Not Excuses: Wake Up, Take Charge, and Overcome Your Financial Fears Forever. New York: Three Rivers, 2008.

Pay It Down! Debt-Free on $10 a Day. New York: Portfolio, 2009.

David Bach

Start Late, Finish Rich: A No-Fail Plan for Achieving Financial Freedom at Any Age (Finish Rich Book Series). New York: Broadway, 2007.

Suze Orman

Suze Orman's Action Plan: New Rules for New Times, rev. ed. New York: Spiegel & Grau, 2010.

FREE Budgeting and Money Management Tool

http://www.mint.com

Online workbook and other resources for
The Prosperity Plan:

www.laurabermanfortgang.com

www.theprosperityplan.net

PO Box 125

Montclair, NJ 07042

(973) 857-8180

To secure Laura B. Fortgang as a keynote speaker, corporate spokesperson or media expert, please contact her at the number above and see clips at www.laurabermanfortgang.com.

INDEX

ABOUT THE AUTHOR

LAURA B. FORTGANG is the author of *Now What? 90 Days to a New Life Direction*, *Living Your Best Life*, and the national bestseller *Take Yourself to the Top*. Her *Little Book on Meaning* was a finalist for a Books for a Better Life Award, alongside works by the Dalai Lama and Pema Chödrön, in 2010. Fortgang is the founder of Now What? Coaching and a cofounder of the International Coach Federation. Her work has been featured in top-tier media in the United States and abroad. As a professional speaker, she has traveled to many corners of the world in an effort to raise consciousness and improve the status quo for individuals, companies, and seekers of all kinds. An ordained interfaith minister, she lives with her husband and three children in Montclair, New Jersey.

Other Laura B. Fortgang titles
available from Tarcher

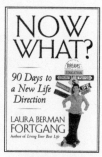

Now What?
90 Days to a New
Life Direction
978-1-58542-413-9

Living Your Best Life:
Discover Your Life's
Blueprint for Success
978-1-58542-157-2

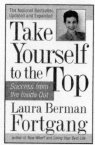

Take Yourself to the Top:
Success from the Inside Out
978-1-58542-447-4

The Little Book on Meaning
Hardcover:
978-1-58542-715-4
Paperback:
978-1-58542-802-1

Unleash your inner winner

with these first-class titles from the

TARCHER MASTER MIND EDITIONS

Over 75,000 copies sold

THE NOW HABIT
ISBN 978-1-58542-552-5

Whether you are a professional, a student, or a homemaker, Neil Fiore, Ph.D., will help you achieve your goals more rapidly—be they large, complex challenges or the small but essential tasks of everyday life and work. The techniques in *The Now Habit* will help all busy people achieve their goals skillfully, and eliminate the anxiety and stress brought on by the workplace's pressing deadlines.

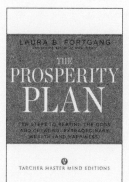

THE PROSPERITY PLAN
ISBN 978-1-58542-856-4

The rules have changed. The old strategies of hard work, fitting in, and loyalty no longer guarantee a secure and shiny future. In *The Prosperity Plan*, Laura B. Fortgang offers a simple and clear approach to building financial and emotional security. This simple ten-step guide will show you how to beat the odds and prosper in ways you never dreamed possible!

Unleash your inner winner

with these first-class titles from the

TARCHER MASTER MIND EDITIONS

THE POWER OF DECISION
ISBN 978-1-58542-854-0

Every great achievement the world has ever seen was born with a single thought. Every great person who ever lived has been a person of decision. Raymond Charles Barker's *The Power of Decision* reveals these principles of success, and illustrates the conscious-minded choices that all of us are capable of making in order to transform our lives and make our dreams come true.

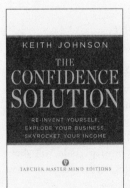

THE CONFIDENCE SOLUTION
ISBN 978-1-58542-865-6

With a blend of his trademark humor, insight, and experience, America's #1 Confidence Coach, Dr. Keith Johnson, shows how all people can achieve their dreams and desires, and realize their full potential. Finally, recognize your inner strengths and talents, boost your confidence, and become a more successful person.